SUCCESS
4LIFE

SUCCESS 4LIFE

THE ENTREPRENEUR'S ODYSSEY

PRESENTED BY

JOSH CADILLAC

JEFF WRIGHT | JAY PEREZ | J.C. DE ONA
JESUS CASTAÑON | TIMOTHY CADILLAC | RAUL RODRIGUEZ
KNOLLY WILLIAMS | CRAIG GRANT

Publishing support provided by
Ignite Press
55 Shaw Ave. Suite 204
Clovis, CA 93612
www.IgnitePress.us

ISBN: 979-8-9992402-0-0
ISBN: 979-8-9992402-1-7 (E-book)

For bulk purchases and for booking, contact:

Josh Cadillac
josh@joshcadillac.com

Library of Congress Control Number: 2025911850

Cover design by K M Shahidul Arafat
Edited by Elizabeth Arterberry
Interior design by Jetlaunch

FIRST EDITION

The Authors

Josh Cadillac
Real Estate Coach, National Speaker, and Author

🌐 close4life.com

📷 instagram.com/joshdcadillac

🌐 acecloser.com

▶️ youtube.com/@joshuacadillac3019

Jeff Wright
Serial Entrepreneur and Negotiator

🌐 therealjeffwright.com

🌐 agentsalesgroup.com

📷 @therealjeffwright

Jay Perez
Husband, Father, Mortgage Pro

🌐 jayrperez.com

🌐 thelendten.com

🌐 mtghelpers.com

J.C. de Ona
Bank Executive

in linkedin.com/in/j-c-de-ona-57418683

Jesus Castañon
CEO & President, Real Estate Empire Group

🌐 instagram.com/realestateempiregroup

◉ instagram.com/jscastanon

🌐 reegroup.com

Tim Cadillac
Speaker, Professor, and Author

in linkedin.com/in/timothycadillac

f facebook.com/tcadillac

Raul Rodriguez

Knolly Williams
The Business Healer

🌐 Knolly.com

▶ youtube.com/user/knollytraining

in linkedin.com/in/knolly

📷 instagram.com/knolly.williams

Craig Grant

CEO of the Real Estate Technology Institute/RETI |

Co-Founder of the BEATS Alliance & BEATS Conference

International Speaker, Trainer, and Tech Evangelist

craiggrant.info

reti.us

beatsconference.com

facebook.com/craiggrantreti

Table of Contents

Introduction

S uccess has no one-size-fits-all formula. It's not something you stumble upon by chance or achieve by copying someone else's path. True success is crafted—inch by inch, lesson by lesson, through trial, grit, and deeply personal transformation.

In *Success4Life: The Entrepreneur's Odyssey*, nine industry leaders invite you behind the curtain of their professional and personal journeys. These are not surface-level wins or highlight reels. Each story is a front-row seat to the mindset shifts, battles, missteps, and victories that shaped their lives—and legacies.

You'll meet entrepreneurs who rebuilt after loss, leaders who chose character over comfort, and visionaries who redefined wealth beyond the numbers. Their experiences span real estate, banking, technology, coaching, sales, and beyond, but what connects them is a commitment to something deeper: living and leading with intention.

These chapters aren't just meant to inspire you—they're meant to equip you. Inside, you'll find actionable insights, unfiltered wisdom, and practical tools to help you navigate your own path to success.

This is your invitation to reflect, recalibrate, and reimagine what success means for *you*. Let these stories challenge you to be more courageous, more authentic, and more aligned with the life you truly want to lead.

Welcome to the odyssey.

CHAPTER 1

Lessons from My Dad

Josh Cadillac

Real Estate Coach, National Speaker, and Author

🌐 close4life.com

📷 instagram.com/joshdcadillac

🌐 acecloser.com

▶ youtube.com/@joshuacadillac3019

Josh Cadillac trains real estate professionals to build lasting success through his Close 4 Life method, which combines industry expertise with the tools to create rapport, credibility, and trust. A top producer since 2008, he quickly earned many of real estate's most prestigious certifications and designations.

He's a nationally recognized speaker and the creator of the ACE series of real estate courses, including the first crypto and real estate course approved for CE in Florida—one of only three nationwide. He was recently honored as Speaker of the Year by Miami Realtors.

● ● ●

"By the inch, it's a cinch, and by the yard, it's hard" was one of my father's favorite sayings. It means that small (inch-sized) changes are easier to make than big ones, but, over time, those "inches" make miles of difference in what you achieve. I want to share some of the small lessons I learned on my journey to success that made a huge difference in getting there.

To understand my route to success, I suppose that tale has to begin with my dad. He was a very smart and successful guy. He had numerous patents, had run several businesses, and despite being a great "big picture" guy, he was also a king of the details. He was a great dad who loved me a lot, but also a tough boss that didn't accept less than my best. He was part of the "Greatest Generation," which means he lived through the Great Depression and World War II, fought in the Korean War, and even went to military school as a kid. He came from the mindset of mental toughness that this generation is famous for, basically, "You beat your head against the wall until the wall gives up." You have to be willing to push through what others can't, won't, or choose not to. Interestingly enough, he never said that to me that way, but he showed me that grit and determination too many times to count.

> By the inch, it's a cinch, and by the yard, it's hard.

My earliest memories are of my dad waking me up very early in the morning to go to open a bagel restaurant he had in North Miami Beach, Florida. I was three years old when he started bringing me, and he taught me how to "open up." I learned where all the light switches were and so that became my first job, running around to turn on all the lights. Little did I know, this small job was the first step in an education my father would give me on how to work. He wanted me to know how to do great work that I took pride in.

My dad was a man of many sayings. He started sharing these "pop-isms" with me as a little boy and never really stopped. These little pieces of wisdom aided more than anything on my journey to success, so I will share a few of them with you here in the hopes they help you on yours:

ALWAYS START A JOB BY TURNING ON THE LIGHTS

"Always start a job by turning on the lights."

That always made sense to me, even as a kid, as before we turned on the lights in the restaurant, we were stumbling around in the dark. It seems so simple, yet all the time, you see adults trying to "save time" by not "turning on the lights."

Dad told me, "you always want to set yourself up to do a job well. It's very hard to do that if you can't see the thing you are working on clearly. We always want to have the lights on before we waste time or do the job poorly, only to have to redo it."

This is a lesson that continues to have a role in my life. Whatever the project is, the first thing I do is make sure I can see clearly what it is I am working on. This could mean making sure we have reports on the business, data, due diligence material, or literally making sure we have adequate lighting for the project. "So, before you start, always turn on the lights."

FAULTY CONSTRUCTION

My dad was always playing the long game with me. He recognized my potential and character flaws. He also had a real sense of his own mortality. His father died when he was only 48 years old, and he was older than that when I was born. He didn't want to leave me unprepared for a world he knew firsthand could be very cruel and unforgiving to the naïve and unhardened. This means that, as much as my dad loved me, he never tolerated any kind of participation-trophy type of stuff.

When I was four years old, I would construct something out of Legos and bring it to my dad for approval. He would look over, shake, and flip it, and if anything fell off, he would hand back what I built and say, "Faulty construction."

Despite what the current thinking on this is, and as the visual evidence would seem to confirm, I didn't die. I learned not to turn in subpar or untested work and expect praise for it. I took what I built and shored up the parts that had issues. I would then bring it back to my dad, who would check it, and when it held up, he would say, "Good work."

The net result is that I learned to have my own standards for what I make and to test it to my satisfaction before I turned it in. When you do anything, look at it and ask if you are just making something that looks good and will pass the visual test, or you are making something that truly is good and even better than how it appears. Because I do this, people that work with me know that if they give me a project, they never have to question the quality of what I bring back. My dad taught me this because he wanted me to have an internal sense of quality. When you do this, people that depend on you will never greet your work with "faulty construction."

SOMETIMES YOU NEED TO LEARN TO SOLDIER

I remember when I was driving with my father to do something that was important, and on the way, I told him that I needed to use the bathroom. He told me, "Son, sometimes you need to learn to soldier." There was no pulling over to find the nearest restroom. No guilt later that he made his son have to be uncomfortable. I learned that day that sometimes, there are things more important than my needs in the moment.

This mindset prepared me for when meals and bathroom breaks sometimes had to be missed during ongoing jobs because something needed to get done and no one thought it could be done. That is when me and my guys would get it done, because we were willing to do what others were not. Learning "how to soldier" was preparation for winning battles with myself later when I needed more than I thought I could give. I demand more of myself, and have surprised myself many times as I exceed what I thought was my maximum capacity. You discover these things when you recognize that "sometimes you need to learn to soldier."

Practicing "learning to soldier" meant building in an extra gear you go to when things need a higher level of effort. This is not how to work all the time, as you can burn yourself out. It does mean learning and practicing doing hard things when you can, so that when hard times come (which they inevitably do) you are prepared to meet them. In practice, that means not always giving in to yourself, but at times pushing and testing your limits. There is a reason why athletes do this, and it is to see what that better version of you looks like and to earn the associated confidence from having endured hard things. By practicing this intermittently, you will find yourself much better suited to handling adversity, and folks that can do that are always in demand.

YOU HAVE TO SET AN EXAMPLE

My childhood was amazing but very short. My dad decided when I was finished with fourth grade that I would be homeschooled in the afternoons and work from 6 AM to 1 PM every day. Luckily, there was an exception to the child labor laws that lets children work in the family business, and I also got a paycheck, which didn't suck either. That is when my career in business started, and it hasn't stopped since. It is one of the best things my father ever did for me, as I got to participate in what went into taking care of our family.

I started out as a storeroom clerk and would load the vending machines at the school cafeteria operation we ran. My dad would always tell me, "You are the boss's son, and people will take their lead from you." If you are lazy, it gives employees an excuse to be lazy as well.

My father knew the importance of leadership and realized that, as an entrepreneur, he could give me opportunities to learn how to lead in a safe environment. Around the time I turned 13, my father had a crew of men and decided to put me in charge. To be clear: I was 13, and these were grown men. The field was ripe for animus and feelings of nepotism to be exercised. My father told me that I needed to show the men I was worthy of the position. I needed to work harder than they did. When they showed up in the morning, I had to already be there, working, and when they left, I would still be plugging away. He said, "people will follow you if you act in a way that is worthy of respect. You are the boss's son and you have to set an example."

To begin with, I thought that meant being better prepared and having all the answers. That led to me not listening and coming off to my crew as insecure. That didn't get me the respect that is so critical for a leader to have. It turned out it was about having an awesome plan, great standards, and being true to your word, but also having the confidence to listen and adjust the plan to what your team suggests. If what they suggested was better, then that was what we did. This made for better morale amongst the team and garnered more respect for me as the guy leading.

There are many stories I could tell about this, but one that comes to mind was the first time we did this major outdoor catering event. We hadn't done this particular event before and the rest of my family was going out of town. Most of my best people were also unavailable. I was left with just two people to pull this off. I worked for weeks before to come up with a plan, layout, and even drawings for what we would do. We started setting up early, around 7 AM, for this 5 PM event. It required a lot of new equipment, and many things we were doing for the first time, that all took much longer than we thought. The team had some great suggestions, though, and we changed several things that netted us a better setup than what I had envisioned. We finished setting up right before the service, and by the time the chaos was over at 9 PM, we were ready for a body bag.

Unfortunately, what goes up must come down. We couldn't leave all of the equipment dirty or outside, so we needed to clean up. We finished at 3 AM, but because I worked the way I was taught, our small team pulled it off, and we still liked each other enough to go to a 3 AM breakfast at a 24-hour diner together. Whenever I see those folks again, this is one of the "war stories" they always love to bring up: how we survived the first roundup. Being a good example and having a good attitude had my team following me because they saw I was not asking them to work any harder than I was willing to.

Those are not all of my father's lessons. Not even close. But these are some of the ones that continue to manifest in my business, and I contend were integral to the success I was able to achieve. You see, my father was teaching them to me not just because he feared dying young. My father always would tell me the stories of fathers that left their families a financial legacy, only to see the children squander it. He didn't want that to happen to us. That was one of his biggest fears, and it was one that was well-founded, it turns out.

My father passed away in 2002, at the age of 72. I was 23 years old, my brother was 21, and my sister was just 12. This was a big hit, because my dad was always the boss. One of the last things he told me when he knew he didn't have much time left was, "You take care of your mother, brother, and sister." It was the last thing I ever remember him asking me to do, and because he was the boss, it was exactly what I tried to do.

In fact, I grew the family business in all sorts of ways, all the time trying to be careful not to over-leverage. Then 2008 came along and wiped us out. I lost everything and had to deal with the guilt and shame of that failure. I had little to work with, but I still had my dad's lessons. He learned these things by building a fortune. Maybe they would work in rebuilding one.

You see, there is one more lesson I didn't mention, which is, when the shit hits the fan, you don't complain, you ask the question, "What the hell are you going to do about it?" He taught me to act. To see what the next thing that needed to be done was and to do it. I asked myself what I knew I could do to help the family. The answer was real estate. My father had spent years teaching me how and now it was time to soldier.

I ran my restaurants with almost no staff and simultaneously got my real estate license. I entered the industry in 2008, in the epicenter of the housing market meltdown. Prices were in free fall and no one was buying. I went to work with an amazing broker and friend named Drew Epstein, who took me under his wing. The change in the market meant that tons of agents left the business. I went to the office every day and picked up all the business those folks left behind. Times got hard, so the folks that didn't know how to deal with discomfort left. Luckily for me, I had been taking AP classes at the "Bob Cadillac School of Business" on this for years.

The market was different than any we had seen before, so we needed to get the full picture. This meant stopping and turning on the lights. The thing the market needed was a way to help folks that were losing their homes get out without having to go through a foreclosure. The answer was short sales. I quickly became an expert on them. My dad's lesson of starting with the lights on meant I had to learn everything I could to understand how they worked. This meant tons of classes, as well as asking anyone else who knew anything about them how short sales worked. Not only did I need to know the processes, legalities, and pitfalls, I also had to learn how to explain them to desperate and emotional sellers. I was able to help people out of unsustainable situations and then, a few years later, get them back in homes to take advantage of one of the best appreciating markets ever. I was able to make money by doing a good thing.

To do this, though, I was showing up to the office no later than 9 AM every day, six days a week, and staying late. My father had taught me to see what everyone else was doing and work smarter and, when necessary, harder than them. I tried to outpace the other agents I saw who were successful. The way my dad taught me to work, by setting an example, attracted all sorts of business and connections. I started collaborating with my business partner Cody Lampariello on the first ACE course and the book *Roadmap to the American Dream* in the evenings after work.

From our work in distressed assets, we were able to start getting access to the non-performing loan market and other distressed assets, which allowed us to buy properties at deep discounts and raise capital to buy more. We would end up owning dozens of income-producing properties. The course we wrote introduced me to a passion of mine: teaching agents. We also founded a property management company, construction company, roofing company, and an investment group.

I eventually met Jesus Castañon, who wound up becoming more than just a friend and business partner—he is also a co-author of this book. He challenged me to create more classes. I listened, and the one class I had turned into 48, which I now teach all over the world. These classes are the result of finding all the "faulty construction" in how real estate and investing is done and taught and addressing it. Figuring out how to fix what doesn't stand up to pressure gave me the tool set to build the education business I have.

All of this has come together to give me great prosperity and a family that loves to be together. My brother is a college professor, my sister just welcomed her first baby into the world, and my mom—well, I'm taking momma to Paris and England this year, after we went to Rome and Venice last year. That seemed so impossible when 2008 happened to us. This is what my hard work has bought me, as well as the ability to know that I was able to fulfill the last request my father gave me. That is real success to me.

In application, this means:

"By the inch, it's a cinch, by the yard, it's hard."

Decide where you want to go, and start making consistent, small changes to who you are to get closer to who you want to be. This means if you want to start going to the gym, go twice a week for 20 minutes for a while to build the habit, and then increase from there. If you want to read more, and don't like to, don't commit to reading a chapter a day. Read a page a day, minimum. This sets reachable goals, builds habits, and sets up a pattern of winning against your lesser self. That is something you can celebrate.

What do you want to be more like?

_____

What can you do today to be more like that?

_____

"Always start a job by turning on the lights."

Take a step back from what you are doing to see how you are doing it. Whether it be how you work, how you manage your finances, or even how you raise your kids, put yourself in position to see what is needed and, then, plan how to make that happen. You can do this by stepping back and observing, asking friends, reading books, meditation, or prayer. Stop stumbling around just doing things to get them done. Turn on the lights, get a good look at the job, and then make a plan of attack.

I need to get better clarity on:

_____

This is how I will get perspective:

_____

"Faulty construction."

Don't turn in crap and accept a gold star for it. I know, for some people, they are their own worst critic, and that is not for you. If your self-criticism is paralyzing you, that is cheating you out of what you could be. A pursuit of excellence, not perfection, is a healthier way to see the kind of greatness you are capable of.

We do live in a world, though, where folks are encouraged to do less than their best, call it their best, and then celebrate less than what they could have made. They are also cheating themselves out of what they could be. Be the person that looks at their work, finds the flaws, and improves them. People like that can be trusted, are always in demand, and are always compensated well because they are hard to find.

This is something I am doing I could be doing better:

_____

This is how I will make it better:

_____

"Learning to soldier."

Caution: This has to be done carefully. You do this when you are not overloaded to build within your capacity. If you do this when you are already overtaxed, you will burn out. This is the little voice in the gym that says "one more set" or "one more rep." This pushes you to find out how good you could be. It starts with the tremendous hope: "you haven't seen your best yet" and pushes you to get closer to it. This also prepares you for when there are hard times, as you have built in that "extra gear" when you need it.

This is an area I can challenge myself in:

_____

Do I have the bandwidth available to handle pushing now?

_____

This is what success looks like:

_____

"Setting an example."

In life, we get the opportunity to lead people sometimes, but the one person we always have to lead is ourselves. By setting a good example for others, I also do so for myself, and this helps to improve my self-respect. Having this improves your confidence and makes people want to work with and for you. Find someone to model yourself after and push yourself to exceed what they do. Imagine someone you want to impress is watching you and work that way. _You_ are watching, and you deserve to see your best.

What is a way you can push yourself to set an example?

_____

Those are some of the smallest lessons that made the biggest difference in my life. Guess those inches really did add up.

CHAPTER 2

The Art of Shutting The F*ck Up

How Strategic Silence Can Save You in Life, Love, and Business

Jeff Wright

Serial Entrepreneur and Negotiator

therealjeffwright.com

agentsalesgroup.com

@therealjeffwright

Jeff Wright is a serial entrepreneur who came from nothing to build Agent Sales Group, an insurance marketing company with a force of 32,000 agents, generating a half billion dollars a year in sales. His fuel has always been taking ownership and not blaming anyone for his lot in life. His book, *Blame to Fame*, has helped many people take ownership of and grow their lives.

He grew up in a home ruled by an alcoholic father. The damage wasn't just loud nights—it was the silence that followed. Shame, guilt, and false beliefs took root and stayed long after the drinking stopped.

Now, he speaks openly about alcoholism—not for attention, but because he knows what it's like to carry those scars. Most who reach out to him are women stuck in toxic dynamics with alcoholics—partners, parents, exes. They want clarity, strength, and peace. The lessons and principles he learned dealing with addicts also apply to sales and negotiations, their use spanning from the boardroom to the bedroom.

His work helps you get your mind back. To stop letting someone else's addiction control your life. To cut the emotional ties without losing yourself in the process. He will show you how to set boundaries, communicate without fear, and move forward—stronger, smarter, and in control.

● ● ●

"Most people do not listen with the intent to understand;
they listen with the intent to reply."
— Stephen R. Covey

INTRODUCTION

My first marriage went down in flames mostly because I couldn't figure out when to just shut up. You know those conversations that start with, "We need to talk." and end with, "I can't do this anymore!" That was my greatest hit. I talked too much, assumed too much, and listened so little I could've moonlighted as a brick wall.

Then I married a woman from Eastern Europe who barely spoke English. At first, I thought the

> Knowing when to shut the hell up can fix just about everything.

language barrier would sink us. Instead, it saved me. It forced me to stop talking and start listening. And it taught me a life-changing truth:

Knowing when to shut the hell up can fix just about everything.

Let me give you an example. I once found myself neck-deep in an argument that started over something as dumb as who left the garage door open. My wife and I were tired, hungry, and in full "who's right?" mode. You know the kind—where every sentence starts with "You always..." or "You never..." and ends with one of you sleeping on the couch.

She was mid-rant, and I had the perfect comeback locked and loaded. I knew if I dropped it, it'd be a mic-drop moment. But for some reason, I didn't. I just stayed quiet.

Instead of firing back, I looked at her and nodded. Not a sarcastic nod, a real one. Then I said, "You're right. That must've felt really frustrating."

Boom. The entire room shifted. Her shoulders relaxed. She stopped pacing. She just looked at me and said, "Thank you."

We ended up sitting down, talking about her day, and laughing over something random. That could've been a blowout fight, the kind you regret for three days. But because I shut up and listened—like, really listened—we walked out of it stronger.

That moment taught me this: the power isn't in having the last word. The power is in letting someone else feel heard.

This isn't about being passive. It's about learning how to pause, breathe, and let curiosity take the wheel. If you're tired of conversations that turn into combat or deals that go sideways, this one's for you.

WHY NOT SHUTTING UP COSTS YOU BIG TIME

Ever known someone who talks just to hear themselves talk? If not, hate to break it to you. . . it might be you. It used to be me.

I remember one meeting early in my business career where I just couldn't stop talking. It was a negotiation. I was young, hungry, and had something to prove. I walked into that room thinking I needed to sell myself, my ideas, and my plan with nonstop confidence.

So I talked. A lot.

About my experience. About the numbers. About the future. I thought I was killing it. But by the time I finally paused, I noticed something—no one was making eye contact. The room was dead silent, not because they were captivated, but because they'd checked out. One of the investors literally looked at his watch and said, "Let's wrap this."

I didn't get the deal. Not because the offer wasn't good, but because I steamrolled the room. I left no space for conversation, no opportunity for their questions, and no room for them to feel heard or respected.

That day cost me a six-figure opportunity and taught me a lesson I never forgot: if you're the only one talking, you're probably the only one who thinks it's going well.

Arguments. Stress. Burned bridges. All because I couldn't let a little silence hang in the air. And according to science, chronic conflict spikes stress hormones and kills your health. But you don't need a lab coat to know that—you've felt it.

Silence isn't weakness. It's wisdom in action.

The truth is, learning when to shut up isn't just polite—it's survival. Like emotional snake boots. Silence gives space. Space gives clarity. Clarity saves marriages, friendships, and yes, even jobs.

I repeat. . . Silence isn't weakness. It's wisdom in action.

STRATEGIC SILENCE 101

Let's be clear: this isn't about giving the silent treatment. It's not some emotional power move or a way to force someone into submission. No, this is about making a deliberate decision to pause, listen, and create space.

I remember sitting at a dinner with a group of businesspeople, one of whom had a reputation for being. . . well, loud. Dominant. The kind of guy who thought being the smartest meant being the loudest. Halfway through a conversation about a potential joint venture, he asked me a question. But before I could even open my mouth, he answered it himself—then kept going.

Now, old me would've jumped in, corrected him, and made sure my opinion was heard. But I didn't. I just smiled, nodded slowly, and said nothing.

What happened next was magic. The guy stumbled a little. Realized he didn't know as much as he thought. And then? He looked at me and said, "You've been quiet. What do you think?"

And *that* was when I spoke. Calm, clear, direct.

The room shifted. People paid attention because I hadn't been trying to win the room—I let the room come to me.

When you breathe and go quiet, your nervous system calms down. And when you listen—really listen—people start to trust you. Your presence feels safe. That's power. Your nervous system calms down. Your presence feels safe. That's power.

TACTICAL TOOLS FOR SHUTTING UP

Let me tell you about the first time I ever tried putting these tools into play on purpose. I was in a heated conversation with a team member who had made a mistake—an expensive one. My instinct was to lay into him, make sure he knew how badly he'd messed up. But I stopped myself.

Instead, I took a breath. I actually stepped away for ten seconds, came back, and asked, "What happened?"

He started explaining, nervous, expecting me to explode. But I kept quiet. I nodded. I said, "Tell me more."

And he did. He not only owned up to the mistake, but pointed out a flaw in our process that had left the door wide open for it. By the time he finished, we weren't talking about blame—we were talking about solutions. I didn't have to yell. I didn't have to dominate the moment. I just had to listen.

That's when I realized these tools weren't just theory. They're practical. They work. You don't have to be a therapist or a monk. You just need a little discipline.

Here's something else I noticed: when I stopped being the guy who always had to be right, I became the guy people came to with their problems. Not because I had all the answers—but because I made space for their answers. Listening makes you approachable. It makes you a problem solver instead of a blamer. And here's the kicker—the more open people feel around you, the more they share. The more they share, the better quality of information you have. And better information? That leads to better decisions, stronger relationships, and yes—more money.

Listening isn't just a social skill; it's a financial strategy. If you want to increase your income, start by increasing your silence. People aren't looking for someone to bark instructions—they're looking for someone who makes them feel safe enough to figure it out themselves.

Here's your no-fuss playbook:

1. **Take a Breath** – Three deep breaths. Get grounded before your mouth makes a mess.
2. **Check Your Assumptions** – Don't fill in the blanks with your own drama.
3. **Ask Instead of React** – A simple "tell me more" goes a long way.
4. **Listen like It Matters** – Actually hear what they're saying.
5. **Speak with Precision** – Less is more. Say only what's needed.

Pro tip: when in doubt, don't. Let silence do the heavy lifting.

THE POWER OF SILENCE IN REAL LIFE

Let me back up a bit and tell you about something that happened years before I figured all this out. I was running a business that was doing well on paper, but inside, it felt like a pressure cooker. One of my managers—a guy I actually liked—was constantly on edge. Always one word away from blowing up.

One day, during a routine meeting, he snapped. Red in the face, voice cracking, he launched into a full-blown tirade about how the company was going in the wrong direction. I could tell he wasn't just pissed about numbers—this was personal. I wanted to cut him off. Wanted to defend myself. Wanted to prove him wrong.

But instead, I just. . . stopped.

I leaned back in my chair, nodded, and said, "Sounds like you've been holding that in for a while. Keep going."

He froze. Blinked. Then kept talking.

For twenty minutes, he spilled everything. His frustrations, fears, what he thought I didn't see, what he was afraid to say. And I just listened. No defense. No clever rebuttals. Just space.

By the time he finished, the tension had left the room. He looked lighter. I looked smarter. And our relationship got stronger—not because I said the right thing, but because I had the sense to say nothing at all.

THE DRUNK BUSINESS ASSOCIATE

Once, a business associate of mine started getting aggressive after going three drinks too deep. He wasn't just being confrontational, he was being theatrical, like he'd watched one too many mob movies. We were seated at a corner table, and while everyone else was trying to enjoy dinner, he leaned in and started slurring threats about what would happen if I didn't play ball.

Old me? I'd have matched his energy, raised my voice, maybe even stormed out or gotten into it right there. But instead, I took a breath. I looked him in the eye and said, "Paint me a picture of what that looks like."

My tone was calm. Even.

He blinked. Paused. Then he kept talking. I followed with, "Tell me more."

He did. And what came out next was a goldmine. He laid out his frustrations, his hidden agenda, his assumptions about me, the whole nine yards. The more I stayed quiet, the more he tried to fill the silence. He practically built a PowerPoint with his words, walking me through his entire angle.

By the end of the night, I knew exactly what his game plan was and how to prepare for it. That conversation—one where I barely said a word—saved me from what could've been a massive financial loss.

That night, I walked away calm, informed—and potentially saved myself millions.

THE $1M HOUSE SALE

Realtors said I was crazy for listing my Clearwater Beach home a million over market. They said it wouldn't appraise, wouldn't attract offers, wouldn't make it past the first week.

But I knew what I had. That deck overlooking the water wasn't just a feature. It was a feeling. And people don't buy square footage, they buy feelings.

When a couple came to tour the house, the woman walked straight through the living room, right past the high-end kitchen, and stepped onto the deck. She stood there in silence, soaking it in.

Then she said, "I could spend the rest of my life out here."

I didn't start pitching. I didn't talk about the recent upgrades or the comps in the neighborhood. I just asked, "What would you do out here?"

She smiled, got misty-eyed, and said, "Drink margaritas. Listen to Jimmy Buffett. Watch the sunset."

I nodded and said, "Coming from South Texas, I bet living on the water feels like a dream."

She looked at me, paused, and started crying. Then she told me her story—about her childhood, her struggles, and how being by the water always brought her peace.

She turned to her husband and said, "Buy it."

She barely looked at the rest of the house. The deal was done on that deck. All I did was ask the right question, then shut up and listened.

Silence doesn't just hold space—it makes space for people to see themselves.

THE LISTENING GAP

Here's the truth: Most people aren't listening. They're just waiting for their turn to talk. They're reloading their next point instead of receiving yours.

And let's be brutally honest—most people don't actually care about *you*. They care about *what's in it for them*. That's not cynical, it's human nature. If you want to be heard, you have to earn it by first helping them feel heard.

I remember a time I was consulting for a startup. They brought me in to help tighten up their pitch to investors. The founder was brilliant, no doubt, but every meeting was the same—he talked *at* people, not *with* them. No pauses. No questions. Just a barrage of words.

So I asked him to try something different. In the next meeting, I told him to start with a question: "What are you hoping to get out of this meeting today?"

He looked at me like I was nuts. But he did it.

The response was gold. The investor laid out exactly what mattered to him. What he was looking for. What his fears were. The founder spent the rest of the meeting listening, labeling, and reflecting back. He barely pitched at all.

They got the deal.

People want to feel understood, not corrected. Validated, not analyzed. Seen, not solved. And the fastest way to give them that? Shut up and listen with curiosity.

Use emotional labels:

- "It sounds like that really affected you."
- "It looks like this is important to you."
- "It feels like you've been holding onto this for a while."

When people feel understood, they open up. And when they open up, they give you everything you need—connection, insight, trust. You don't need to be a genius. Just be present.

WHAT *NOT* TO DO

Never Ask Why

Let's settle this now: **never ask why** when you're trying to truly understand someone.

Why? Because "why" questions almost always sound accusatory—even if you don't mean them that way. Think about it. "Why did you do that?" or "Why are you upset?" instantly puts the other person on the defensive. Their brain hears it as: *You messed up, explain yourself.*

Now compare that to:

- "What happened that led to this?"
- "How did that make you feel?"

See the difference? "What" and "how" create space. "Why" corners people. One opens a door. The other slams it shut.

It's a subtle shift with massive impact. Next time you're tempted to ask someone *why* they did something, pause. Reframe. You'll get better answers and fewer walls.

Let me give you a quick example of what not to do—because I've done it all. I was once in a conversation with a colleague who clearly had something on their mind. Instead of asking what was going on, I started giving advice. Not requested advice. Not helpful advice. Just rapid-fire suggestions.

Every time they tried to speak, I cut them off with another "solution." It didn't take long for them to shut down. Their body language changed. They crossed their arms, leaned back, and gave me that tight-lipped smile that says, "Are you done yet?"

Afterward, someone else from the team came to me and said, "They were actually going to tell you something important. But you didn't give them the chance."

Lesson learned.

Sometimes being helpful means shutting up. Sometimes clarity means silence. People need space to feel heard before they'll ever care about what you have to say.

Do This	Not That
Take a breath	Jump to conclusions
Ask a clarifying question	Assume you're right
Reflect back what they said	Interrupt with your story
Label emotions carefully	Tell them how they should feel
Let silence settle	Fill it with nervous babbling

ONE *NO* IS WORTH TWO DOZEN *YESES*

Here's a truth most people miss: a clear, honest **no** is often more valuable than a polite, sugar-coated yes. Why? Because when someone says no, they're telling you the truth. They're giving you a boundary. They're showing you where the edges are—and that's something you can work with.

Yeses, especially the fake kind, lull us into false security. They tell us what we want to hear but not what we need to know. I'd rather get a clean no and know where I stand than chase 24 yeses that lead to nowhere.

In negotiation, in sales, in relationships—one honest no clears the fog. It forces clarity. It eliminates the guessing games.

Here's the kicker: most people want to say no anyway. It makes them feel safe. It makes them feel in control. So why not let them?

Instead of asking, "Do you have a few minutes to talk?" which pressures someone into a yes, try, "Is now a bad time to talk?" Now they get to say no, feel good about it, and you've just earned trust without forcing a fake yes.

Instead of, "Would you like to hear more about our offer?" try, "Would it be ridiculous to explore a better option together?"

That little shift gives people psychological safety. They feel like they're opting in—not being sold to. A confident no is better than a hesitant yes any day.

So next time you hear a no, don't flinch. Lean into it. Ask, "What would need to be true for that to turn into a yes?" You'll get more honest dialogue, more real direction, and far better results. It forces clarity. It eliminates the guessing games.

FINAL CHALLENGE

In your next high-stakes moment—at home, at work, or anywhere in between—try this:

- Breathe.
- Ask.
- Listen.
- Say less than you want to.

Try one conversation this week where you say half as much as you normally would. See what happens. Don't fill the silence. Let it pull something deeper from the person across from you.

> Silence isn't empty. It's full of answers. Let it do the talking.

I remember doing this during a tense client negotiation. There was a moment where everyone expected me to jump in, to clarify or defend our position. But I stayed silent. Not in a passive-aggressive way— just open, calm, and curious. And sure enough, the client kept talking. Within minutes, they revealed a fear they hadn't admitted to anyone else in the room. That changed the whole direction of the deal. We addressed the real concern and walked out with a signed contract. Not because I spoke, but because I didn't.

You'll be amazed at what people reveal when you stop trying to impress and start being curious.

Silence isn't empty. It's full of answers. Let it do the talking.

CHAPTER 3

I'd Rather Lose Money than My Reputation

Lend Ten Principle #3: Accountability Isn't Optional

Husband, Father, Mortgage Pro

 jayrperez.com

 thelendten.com

 mtghelpers.com

Jay R. Perez, founder of Mortgage Helpers and Unlimited Funding Solutions, is a seasoned mortgage professional who has blended grit, knowledge, and integrity into a 20-year career in a highly competitive and fast-paced industry. Raised by a single mom in Miami, Jay inherited a relentless work ethic and his father's gift of gab, propelling him from humble blue-collar roots to industry prominence. Starting in telecom, he broke sales records at Nextel before diving into mortgages in 2005, navigating a volatile economy to master the trade. In 2022, as co-leader of a top-ranked team at PRMG, Jay foresightfully recognized the need to pivot before the market's shift and went into business for himself.

A first-generation Cuban-American, Jay broke cycles of struggle, shaping a boutique and bespoke approach that empowers prominent Hispanic small business owners and tradesmen with tailored lending solutions. His book distills a journey of personal growth and professional reinvention inspired by his evolution from the "nice guy" to a confident leader, guided by mentors, his life experience, and a quiet confidence that reminds everyone not to "forget about Jay." Jay lives in Miami with his wife, Joanna, three kids, and four dogs, chasing a legacy of impact and excellence.

This is what I get for not working with you!" Daniela says to me, frustrated out of her mind.

It's the kind of call every loan officer dreads—but secretly enjoys. One of your favorite agents just watched a deal fall apart because she didn't use you. And she knows it.

"Remember that client that came with his own lender? I called you around Christmas because I was worried that guy was taking too long to start the file?"

"Yeah," I replied, concerned. "What happened?"

"I forgot to extend the finance contingency, and now the agent wants to take his $5,000 deposit."

"Damn, D. . . That sucks," I said, guilt creeping in for indulging her pain.

She wasn't finished. "The other lender was dragging his feet and never ordered the appraisal until the client filed his taxes at the end of January. By the time he did, the appraisal came back short—*big time*. And guess what?"

She didn't wait for a response.

"The contingency had passed. Now they're keeping the deposit. I missed it. I messed up. I know it's on me! But I told Tony, 'This wouldn't have happened if I was working with Jay. There's no way Jay would've let this happen.' I swear, this is the last time I work with another lender."

"D, you're absolutely right," I said with a half-chuckle.

I wasn't laughing at her—I was just acknowledging a truth we both understood. That wouldn't have happened on my watch. And she knew it.

"I'm not going to let my client lose $5,000," she added. "I'll give it to him myself if I have to. Either way, I'm sending you the client. I'm done with that guy."

"You never, *never* leave your wingman."

Letting the finance contingency lapse on a contract is like leaving your wingman—a course of action famously condemned in one of the greatest movies of all time, *Top Gun*.

No matter whether it's our first deal or our fiftieth, if we're in contract together, we're flying the same mission: protecting our client.

Daniela and Anthony of DA Luxury Group are rising stars in one of Miami's hottest firms. I've worked with them for a while now, and during that time, we've grown close. I've naturally taken on a brotherly role, helping them navigate the challenges of giving your all to your career while balancing life.

And in this situation—like so many others—it all comes down to accountability.

Could you argue it wasn't her fault? Sure. Maybe the lender should've been proactive. Maybe the client shouldn't have signed a contract before filing taxes. There's plenty of blame to go around. But to us, there's no gray area. She owned it. She was accountable. And she was willing to take a $5,000 hit to protect her client. That's what sets her apart. That's why I know she'll be successful.

Over the last twenty years, I've seen agents and mortgage LOs come and go, and there's a common thread among the ones who last: they stand for something.

Those who don't? They're in it for the money. And eventually, that shows.

Through all the ups and downs since 2005, I can honestly look back and proudly say I've lived by a set of core principles. They've helped me build a career that allows me to walk into any room knowing that, even if I may not be the best mortgage guy in there, there aren't many better.

These principles helped me stand out by committing to a level of professionalism that's hard to find. That's why Daniela called me. She knew this wouldn't have happened on my watch.

Why?

Because she knows one of the core principles I live by:

"I'd rather lose money than my reputation."

I know I didn't invent this concept. And I'm not claiming to be the first to build a business around values. But I've learned that *living* this stuff—really living it—is rare. Saying it is easy. Standing on it when it costs you? That's a different level. That's what separates people like Daniela—and hopefully me—from the rest.

"WAS IT INSTINCT—OR INFLUENCE?"

You might be wondering where I got this obsession with accountability.

It goes way back—to 2002—when I was just a kid slinging phones at a Nextel store. Before the iPhone, Nextel was king. That's where I met Bryan.

We went to the same high school and shared a lot of the same friend groups. Bryan was raw talent—cocky, charming, immature, but undeniably sharp. The kind of guy who could sell anything.

The next morning, after Bryan covered our store, a client I previously helped came back needing help with the phones Bryan sold him. Standard sales floor ethics said: if someone helped a client, they got the credit. Bryan didn't follow that rule. He rang the deal under his number.

I called him. Told him I was reversing the order. I said, "Don't do that again."

Most guys would've taken that personally, but Bryan respected it.

That became the foundation of our friendship. Quiet competition. Mutual growth. He'd throw jabs like, "What, you think you're gonna be assistant manager or something?"

"Yeah," I said. "I am."

And a few weeks later—I was.

After that, I watched *him* get lit up by a new fire around that time. His uncle, a successful financial planner, got him into Zig Ziglar. Personal development. Motivation. Sales philosophy.

He leveled up—fast.

Soon after, Bryan asked, "What did you do to get promoted?"

I said, "Simple. Do your job—and pick up the slack."

That line stuck. Within 30 days, he got promoted. Another 30 days, and he was a store manager. He was a natural. People gravitated to him. He had the gift.

And then, one day, a title agent told him: "You'd kill it in mortgages."

She handed him a card. He followed up.

Soon after, he became a mortgage broker and started pulling me with him. I eventually left Nextel and joined Ameriquest—one of the largest subprime lenders at the time and the first domino to fall in the 2008 mortgage crash.

Eventually, I joined Bryan at his brokerage. I brought the structure and process I'd learned at Ameriquest. He brought his charisma and drive. Together, we were building something strong. He was the face. I was the engine.

Until everything fell apart.

TWO ROADS, ONE STANDARD

By mid-2007, the crash hit. I left the business.

At that point, my life was changing fast. I had just met Johanna, a recently divorced mom with two beautiful kids, Cameron and Anthony. I went from bachelor to father figure overnight. My vision shifted. Bryan's didn't.

We stayed friends, but it was clear our paths were diverging.

Though I had talent, I didn't yet have the experience or confidence to navigate those times. I burnt out. I stayed home, depressed. Lost. Until, one day, Johanna sat me down and said:

"Stop feeling sorry for yourself. Go get a job."

I credit her for lighting that fire. That hard truth became one of the biggest turning points of my life.

Fast forward to late 2011. Bryan and I reconnected.

He seemed different—engaged, focused, calm. He had weathered the worst of the storm and made some good connections along the way. Dodd-Frank had just passed. There were signs the market was coming back.

We had dinner with his fiancée and my wife, and everyone agreed—maybe it was time to finish what we started.

So I quit my job and went back to work with Bryan as his assistant.

That's when the curtain lifted.

Almost immediately, I realized things weren't as they seemed. Bryan wasn't licensed under the new mortgage laws. He was running deals through a friend "while his attorney figured it out."

At first, I didn't fully get it. But the red flags piled up—fast.

Bryan still had the gift—he could sell anything. But he was chaotic. He'd lock in a deal, make promises, then disappear when the hard part came. I called it "dropping grenades and leaving the room."

That left me:

Fielding agent calls. Calming clients. Doing damage control.

Johanna would see the stress and ask me, "Why do you care so much? Those are *his* problems."

But I knew the truth.

Bryan, for all his flash, was broke. Living check to check. If I didn't fix the problem, I wouldn't get paid.

I was doing this not because I wanted to, but because I had to.

I told Johanna, "It's teaching me the job. If he can't get his act together, I'll just do it myself."

And that's exactly what happened.

I learned a lot from Bryan—mainly what **not** to do!

Bryan's philosophy was: "Never accept responsibility—just figure out who to blame."

That's why he burned bridges. That's why he plateaued. That's why his reputation eventually caught up with him.

Me? I chose the opposite.

> "I'd rather lose money than my reputation."
> —*Accountability Isn't Optional*

WHEN ACCOUNTABILITY BECOMES STRATEGY

In today's fast-paced, commission-chasing real estate and mortgage world, accountability is often the first thing to go.

It's easier to point fingers. Blame the system, the buyer, or the processor. But the real pros—the ones who *last*—put their money where their mouth is. They stand behind their advice and decisions.

You don't need catastrophe to show it. The magic's in the small moments.

Here's an example that's played out a thousand times.

> "I'd rather lose money than my reputation."
> —*Accountability Isn't Optional*

Agents are unsure about the value. Maybe it's tricky or maybe they're new. Either way, what do most people do?

They proceed and hope the appraisal hits. After all, if they don't try, there's no deal. It's a risk they're willing to take—but the bigger question is: what expectations do they set with the client?

Good agents let the client decide whether to move forward.

Bad agents? They keep quiet and blame the appraiser when it comes in short.

Here's where I'm different: I offer an "appraisal assurance."

What does that mean? If appraisal doesn't hit and the deal falls apart, I cover the next appraisal.

Not a "credit at closing"— cold, hard cash upfront.

Why? Because if I'm asking my client to take a risk, I should be willing also.

One might say, "But you're the loan officer. That's the agent."

Maybe. But here's the way I see it:

I chose the lender. The lender chooses the appraisal company that assigns the appraiser. That whole chain starts with *my decision.*

Now don't get me wrong—I'm not offering refunds on every deal that doesn't work out.

I use appraisal assurance to set clear expectations from the start.

1. If I'm asking you to risk $600–$700, shouldn't I be willing to risk the same?
2. It removes pressure from the agent and shows I've got their back.
3. It humanizes the process for the client—and helps them start trusting the team more.

One may say, "That's genius." Or. . . "You're a sucker."

Have I paid for my fair share of appraisals? Yes. But far fewer than you'd think.

That is peanuts when I compare how many times it helped me close a sale against how many times I've actually had to pay out.

The truth is, conviction isn't about what others think. It's about what *you* think.

Every time I've offered—and delivered—it's been met with appreciation.

When you take accountability from others, that reliability becomes your reputation, your brand. And your brand is your legacy.

BUILT ON MORE THAN MARKETS

If you've ever played high-level sports or developed any skill that separates you from the crowd, then you know: there's no better feeling than being validated by someone you respect.

Unlike Daniela, who had been in the business for a few years and crossed over from mortgages into real estate, Anthony (her business partner) was just getting serious about real estate after a few years in life insurance. For New Year's, they made a plan: Daniela would go after Miami's red-hot luxury market, and Tony would aim for the commercial market—one of the hardest spaces to break into.

To level up, they joined one of Josh Cadillac's famous Ace Investor Courses—part of what's made Josh one of the most respected real estate educators in the country.

I'll never forget Tony's call during his lunch break at that first class.

"Bro. . . You're Josh's mortgage guy? I knew we made the right call."

He was buzzing. And honestly? So was I.

As much as Tony felt validated by working with Josh and choosing the right circle, I felt validated knowing that my work had earned that kind of trust in rooms like that.

That moment meant even more than Tony probably realized.

I had just opened my own brokerage. I was rebuilding. Reinventing.

For the previous eight years, I had been a branch manager at one of the top mortgage companies in the country. I started as a loan officer in 2014 and, by my final month in 2022, was leading the top-producing branch in the company. I had it all—a strong team, industry accolades, consistency, and a great life. But after the wild COVID boom, I sensed a storm coming. I tried to stay ahead of it—changed companies, shifted my role—but the move backfired.

I lost traction, momentum, and confidence.

I was no longer the guy at the top of the mountain. I was at the bottom, starting over—again.

But that's when I realized something: I had been living by a code the whole time. I just never called it one.

When I was given the opportunity to be part of *Success4Life* and looked at my coauthors, it really was a humbling feeling. It put the last 20 years in perspective. How did I get here?

I remember something Bryan told me when we started out: "This business is lonely. The only thing that makes you feel better is your bank account."

In the early years, that stuck with me more than I care to admit. My personal ambitions—being a loving husband, a strong father, providing for my family, giving my kids the life I never had—were always at the center. But my definition of success? It defaulted to material things.

I wasn't flashy, but I told myself I wouldn't buy a Rolex until I reached a place where the cost didn't even matter. And for my 40th birthday, I did just that. I had just closed my largest commission to date—multiple six figures—and looked at my wife and said, "I'm ready for my Rolex."

It wasn't about the watch. It was about what it represented.

I had checked every box:

- A loving home and family — ✅
- Professional accolades and awards — ✅
- Investment properties — ✅
- Waterfront vacation home with the boat — ✅
- Dream sports car — ✅

I was 40. I had built what I thought was the dream.

And then. . . I felt empty.

I remember telling my wife, "I never thought I'd get here. But now that I'm here. . . What's next?"

Funny how God always has an answer to that question.

Within the next three years, I found myself returning from a birthday getaway feeling defeated. The post-COVID market shift hit our model hard. Interest rates spiked. The business slowed. Once again, I was starting over.

Now don't get me wrong—I still had my family, my home, and the "stuff." I had saved well. But something was missing.

I felt like I had built it all. . . for nothing.

And just like she did back in 2008, my wife stepped in with the truth I needed to hear—only this time, from a place of wisdom:

"It wasn't for nothing. You did it without a reputation the first time. Now you've got one. Do it again, with that."

That hit me hard. She was right.

Back in 2008, I left the business because I lacked the confidence and maturity to handle the chaos. But now? I was different. I had built a name for myself. I had the body of work. I had earned the trust of my clients, partners, and peers.

And with that came a deeper kind of confidence—the kind that isn't built on titles or commissions, but on knowing exactly who you are and what you value.

It wasn't the end. It was a new beginning.

For the first time, I wasn't chasing the next goal—I was driven by something more meaningful.

I realized that my true purpose wasn't just to succeed, but to help others do the same. To use everything I had learned—the wins, the losses, the rebuilds, and the resets—to guide others toward a path built on integrity, not just income.

That's the mission I'm on now.

"I'd rather lose money than my reputation" is just one of ten core values I live by—a part of a larger framework I call "The Lend Ten."

But no matter how strong your principles are, no one succeeds alone.

I'm grateful to Josh Cadillac not just for the opportunity to share my story here, but for being the kind of friend who's held me accountable, encouraged me through the hard seasons, and reminded me that integrity always wins.

If you've ever felt like you were navigating this business—or life—on your own, I hope my chapter reminds you: you're not.

We all need people who push us to be better. People who remind us of who we are when we forget.

That's what *Success4Life* is about.

And that's the kind of circle in which I'm proud to participate.

CHAPTER 4

The Art of Distinction

J.C. de Ona

Bank Executive

linkedin.com/in/j-c-de-ona-57418683

J.C. de Ona was born and raised in Miami, Florida. He currently lives in Coconut Grove with his wife and two sons. J.C. attended Florida International University, where he received his bachelor's in finance and his master's in business administration.

J.C., a career banker, has been in banking for 28 years. He has worked in various roles in bank retail, operations, private banking, commercial lending, real estate, construction, and executive management. J.C. is currently president of Centennial Bank's Southeast Florida division.

J.C. currently sits on the board of the Li'l Abner Foundation, Ronald McDonald House Charities, and the South Florida Regional Transportation Agency. He previously served as chairman for March of Dimes events and was a member of Florida International University's Honors College Board.

J.C. received the 40 Under 40 award from the South Florida Business Journal, which recognizes the top 40 business professionals under the age of 40. He has also received Up and Comer awards in banking from Lifestyle Media Group and South Florida Business and Wealth, which recognizes the top business professionals in South Florida. J.C. was also the recipient of the Apogee Award from South Florida Business and Wealth, which recognizes C-suite leaders whose dedication to their industries and communities deserves recognition.

• • •

A s I sit on the porch of my vacation home in the Florida Keys, a gentle breeze rustles the palm trees. My wife and two little boys laugh in the background, while my parents, siblings, nieces, and nephews are in the pool, enjoying the day. With a drink in hand, I gaze out at the open water, feeling an overwhelming sense of gratitude. This moment is the ultimate success—being surrounded by loved ones, enjoying the fruits of my labor, and reflecting on the journey that brought me here.

I was born and raised in Miami, Florida, to parents who emigrated from Cuba. Growing up in a hardworking, middle-class family, I learned the value of dedication and perseverance early on. My humble beginnings instilled in me a drive to work hard and aim high, shaping the path that would lead me to where I am today.

While studying finance at Florida International University, I took a part-time job as a teller at a bank. This was my first real step into the world of finance and banking, where I quickly immersed myself in the operations and culture of the industry. Working hard in this role, I observed how the bank functioned and began to envision a future for myself within this field. It opened a door, allowing me to see if it was something I liked and wanted to continue as a career with a path of growth.

I quickly excelled as a teller and soon had the opportunity to take on greater roles like account representative. Standing out among my peers, I quickly became a young star. I realized that doors open when the spotlight is on you, and you have to move quickly to take advantage of any opportunities. I worked smart and created good relationships with coworkers and clients. I set goals early on to make sure I was noticed.

While working in my first role in banking, I found myself drawn to a group of investment advisors who were not only successful but clearly enjoyed their work. Their professionalism, which was evident in their attire, cars, and camaraderie, inspired me to look beyond my current role. I wanted to have that success. The fancy suits, nice cars and watches, and the way they were respected were all aspects of their bearing I admired. As a young man, this made a big impression on me. I imagined myself being one of those guys, one day. I put it in my mind to get there. This aspiration led me to explore investment advisory and financial markets more.

I seized an opportunity to work for a smaller bank where I could absorb new facets of banking. Here, I learned from seasoned professionals, gaining insights into the operations and management of retail banking. I always made sure to learn from coworkers who had more years of experience. I made it a point to absorb qualities that I felt were crucial for success.

At this bank, there was a group of bankers that I would say came from a different era in banking, when banking was in its true relationship based form. I felt that this quality was something that was quickly dying. Being a younger banker, I made sure to show my interest in learning from the seasoned professionals. I feel like I brought a younger, more vibrant energy but fit in with their demeanor. I aligned myself with these guys and learned a lot. I was seen by many of them as being almost like a younger brother, or even a son.

I felt like they rooted for me to win. This was a good feeling. It propelled me to show them I was a winner, and to win in a way that would make them proud when I succeeded. After all, I was going to be around longer, and their investment in my success was almost like passing the torch. Relationships became the core of my focus: specifically, how to build relationships that break the barrier of just business and create a deeper, more personal connection. I knew that this would be a key to my future success.

Success at a young age did come with its challenges. I had to learn to deal with coworkers and management that did not like the attention I was getting. Some were clearly envious of my success and relationships built with other management and clients. I played my cards right and did the only thing I thought would keep me going in the direction I wanted *and* keep them at bay: keep being the best in my role and creating stronger relationships.

After graduating from FIU with a bachelor's in finance, I decided to take a job with a bank that gave me the opportunity to expand my banking abilities and take on investment advisory as well. I had not forgotten those guys with the nice suits and fancy cars. I loved the financial markets, and this was a great opportunity for my career. I was able to get fully licensed as an investment advisor, providing both banking and investment advising to clients. In this role, I shined once again, gaining the attention of upper management. I analyzed what everyone was doing and how I could do it smarter and better. If most of my peers were setting up ten meetings a week, I was doing thirty. I didn't stop working at 5 PM. I didn't stop working on the weekends. I was always working. However, I was working at building relationships so I was able to do it anywhere. I worked smart and found a way to enjoy life and do the things I wanted to do while fostering relationships that opened doors.

I could be at the gym in the morning and meet people, then have drinks at night with people from the right circles. I could be at the beach or even a club on the weekend and be fostering relationships while having a good time. I surrounded myself with like-minded people, made friends with people that were ambitious and going places. Making the right friends and being in the right circles makes a huge difference in your life. I cemented myself as the banker in town. I had a goal to become a private banker and, with the spotlight on me as the top banker in my position, I decided to ask for the opportunity to enter private banking. That opportunity was granted, and boy did it take me to the next level.

As a private banker, the level of respect I received was greater. The title opened doors for me, allowing me to build upon the relationships I cultivated and help them in so many ways. I was opening doors to a whole new world of individuals, from successful entrepreneurs to influential and famous athletes and entertainers. Building relationships wasn't just about business; it was about truly understanding people. I took the time to get to know my clients on a personal level, which allowed me to identify those who had potential. It was about recognizing the spark in them, the drive to succeed, and being willing to take a chance on their vision. By standing behind these individuals, I not only helped them achieve their goals but also created a network of loyal, grateful clients who were integral to my own success. This mutual trust and support became a cornerstone of my career.

To truly stand out again, I made an effort to do what others might not be willing to do. This meant being available to clients at all times, whether after hours or on weekends, and going the extra mile to wow them. Sometimes, that involved tasks outside my usual role, like making connections or helping someone in a way that wasn't part of my job description. I did these things not expecting anything in return, simply because it was the right thing to do. This genuine approach helped build trust and respect, showing people that I was someone who truly cared.

As my network grew, so did my ability to offer help, often in unexpected ways. There was one time when I had a client who was really into cars and was looking for a very specific car that was extremely difficult to get. I called a client of mine who was in the auto industry and I knew probably had the ability to get this rare car. Asking for the favor, I was able to get one of the few cars available in the US for my client. I did not have to do this, and I did not benefit financially from it, but my client will never forget that I went out of my way to do them a favor, expecting nothing in return. Years later, they are both still my clients and they have done millions of dollars in business together.

Early on, I recognized the importance of appearance. I made it a point to dress well from head to toe, knowing that first impressions matter. As a young professional speaking with clients who had far more experience and wealth, I wanted to project confidence and sophistication. I even wore glasses instead of contact lenses to add a touch of maturity to my look, which helped bridge the gap between my youth and the seasoned professionals with whom I interacted. This attention to detail in my appearance became a key component in establishing credibility and earning respect in my field.

Projecting success was also important, as many people want to do business with those who appear successful. Even when I was just starting out and still climbing the ladder, I made it a point to drive a nice car, dress well, and carry myself with confidence. This image of success helped open doors and build trust with clients, proving to be a key component in my growth and success.

Alongside projecting success, I constantly envisioned my growth. Visualizing my path to success became a powerful tool, guiding my actions and decisions. By envisioning where I wanted to be, I was able to set clear goals and pursue them with determination. This mindset not only kept me focused but also reinforced my confidence, helping turn my aspirations into reality.

As I progressed in my career, I kept focus on the importance of building strong relationships. I made a point to connect with clients on a personal level, understanding their needs and going the extra mile. This approach not only helped me foster trust, but also allowed me to stand out as someone willing to take calculated risks. I learned to identify and back individuals who showed promise, even when it meant stepping outside traditional boundaries. This willingness to support others paid off, as each relationship I nurtured became a stepping stone in my path to success.

Later in my career, I pivoted from my private banking role into more of a generalist role, where I did more work in commercial and real estate lending capacities. However, the private banking role was still at the heart of everything I did, and all my clients were still being handled as private banking relationships.

The chance to return to it came when I was offered an opportunity to help a newer, smaller bank grow in Miami. It was more of an entrepreneurial chapter in my career. It was a change, and it was challenging. However, it proved to be a great career move. Not only did I continue polishing myself as a banker, but it gave me the opportunity to be part of and engage in larger roles in my career. It was one of those decisions that was a fork in the road. I had made a few institutional moves previously in my career and I had always calculated the right move at the right time. It is crucial to time that spotlight to make a move that is not only the right financial decision but the right career move, and at the right moment. You can't be afraid to make a change because you are comfortable where you are. Stagnation is not good. If you do not see a future where you are, or you are not given the opportunity you deserve, find the better fit. Find an opportunity and shine.

Post-recession, adapting to a shifting environment was crucial. I knew I needed to think outside the box to continue generating business and fostering relationships. By structuring deals in unconventional ways and anticipating the next wave of opportunities, I positioned myself ahead of the curve. By identifying and supporting promising individuals, I was able to navigate this period with innovation and success. At a time when lending was difficult and most banks pulled back, I had a few clients looking to buy distressed notes from banks. I started to call banks to help them find good note buys and structured financing on pools of loans for these clients, which no one was doing at the time. I had another group of clients that had started a fund to look at buying distressed homes in south Florida. I came up with a systematic loan facility which would allow them to buy more homes leveraging their portfolios. This, again, was something that was just not being done at the time. I saw the opportunity when most lenders were just not lending. I believed in my clients and what we were doing. This approach not only set me apart but also brought significant success to the bank. It's okay to go against the grain sometimes. Sometimes, that's where you see your biggest success.

Adapting to changing times is key. Being prepared for that and moving quickly is crucial to any business. The environment is subject to change at any time. I've seen it a few times already. I see more changes coming as we continue to see advancements in technology that will affect just about every industry.

Several years into my career, I decided to go back and get my master's in business. This decision was not only an investment in myself, but also a way to stand out in my field. Not everyone in banking has a master's, so this helped distinguish me further. It expanded my knowledge and allowed me to meet new people and foster new relationships, all of which contributed to my continued growth and success. After working in my field for several years, I believe my experience helped me better understand my roles and apply learned skills to the real world. I also believe I was able to give more value to the classroom through questions asked and knowledge demonstrated.

One of the most valuable skills I developed was discerning who to do business with and who to stand behind. This keen sense allowed me to take calculated risks, backing individuals who showed promise. I made it a point to listen, understand, and truly get to know those I was considering supporting. Every single time I chose to back a particular person turned out to be the right decision, contributing significantly to my career success. This ability to build and maintain strong relationships was pivotal, as it reinforced my reputation as someone who not only took chances but made them count. This did come with some added stress. At times, I may have put myself on the line a bit much, but my gut feeling always prevailed.

From an early age, I held myself to the highest standards. This commitment to integrity, standing by my word, and always doing the right thing became the bedrock of my career. During challenging times like the Great Recession, I didn't turn my back on clients; instead, I picked up the phone, offering my support and assistance. I made it clear that I was there to help, regardless of how long we'd known each other. This unwavering dedication to my clients' well-being and the community built a reputation of trust and reliability. By consistently operating with the highest integrity, I showed people the type of person I am, which has been essential to my long-term success.

Throughout my career, I was never afraid to make bold moves, even when they carried a bit of risk. Trusting my gut was crucial, like when I left a large institution for a smaller, startup bank despite having management offers from more well-known banks. This entrepreneurial leap, based on careful analysis and a gut feeling, turned out to be a tremendous success. I've always taken the time to analyze my surroundings, knowing when to take the right risks that could lead to significant payoffs. This ability to judge and work with the right people has been instrumental in my continued growth, in both a personal and business sense. Even in my current role, after the smaller institution I joined was acquired by a larger bank, I faced many options. My gut feeling was to stay on board, recognizing the potential for growth with the right people and the opportunity to continue serving my existing clients. This decision proved beneficial for both my clients and my career. Working with a great group of people, my intuition once again guided me to the right decision, reinforcing my belief in trusting my instincts.

No matter where you are in your career, you deal with similar things. You learn from your previous decisions. You will always have those that are envious of you and don't like to see you do so well. There are also those that support you. You keep building on your success and surrounding yourself with those that support you.

Now, as a president, I love to help others succeed. I love identifying those that have the fire and helping them cultivate it. The way I see it, the more I can help those around me succeed, the more I succeed. Today, I continue building relationships, both with clients and with coworkers. At work, I love creating a great work environment: building camaraderie, creating a workplace that is fun and that people enjoy. The happier team members are at work, the more energy they are going to put into their work, which equates to a more successful company. These are all things I have picked up along the way, things I absorbed from great people I have worked with in my career, who see things I would have liked to see differently. I continue learning as I go and I always look for ways to improve.

I've built some great relationships over the years. Many of those relationships have resulted in the nurturing of dear friends. Some I don't see as often, but when we get together or talk on the phone, we pick up as if we last spoke yesterday. These bonds are what I hold dearest from my career. Like anything else, there are good days and bad days. There are challenging times and booming times. But I love what I do.

Reflecting on my journey, from my early years as a teller to a bank president today, I see the importance of the art of distinction. It's about standing out, building meaningful relationships, learning to trust your gut, and continuously adapting. Every step, from excelling as a teller to pursuing my master's and making bold career moves, has been about growth, both personal and professional. The key takeaway? Success isn't luck. It's the hard work you put behind it, envisioning your goals and how to accomplish them, and it's about relationships. It's investing in yourself and believing in yourself. It's about enjoying your journey and sharing it with those who matter most.

CHAPTER 5

Overcoming Life's Sharks: Journey from Poverty

Jesus Castañon

CEO & President, Real Estate Empire Group

🌐 instagram.com/realestateempiregroup

📷 instagram.com/jscastanon

🌐 reegroup.com

Jesus Castañon is the CEO and president of Real Estate Empire Group, a top-producing real estate brokerage with offices in Doral, Palmetto Bay, Miramar, Fort Myers, Montego Bay (Jamaica), and Bimini (Bahamas). With over 20 years in the industry and more than $2 billion in closed transactions, Jesus has earned a reputation as one of South Florida's most trusted and accomplished real estate leaders.

He oversees a team of over 500 agents, fostering a culture rooted in integrity, education, and performance. Under his leadership, REEG has grown into a powerhouse firm, serving buyers, sellers, and investors across Florida and the Caribbean. Passionate about agent development, Jesus frequently hosts masterminds and live trainings, and he speaks at industry events to help real estate professionals grow long-term, referral-based businesses.

Despite his professional success, Jesus's greatest pride lies in his role as a husband and father. His family is the foundation of everything he does, fueling his commitment to excellence. Whether mentoring agents or leading expansion, Jesus leads with vision, purpose, and heart.

MY LIFE NOW

So, I'm in a 20-million-dollar helicopter, flying to a private island in the Bahamas with my dear friends. Yes, they are my friends, but these are guys that are worth collectively more than a billion dollars. And we're going to spend the day on the beach, at a beach club overlooking the ocean, having drinks and smoking cigars. I find myself asking, what the fuck am I doing here? What are the sacrifices and choices that got me here? Because those got me to the point where my real estate career, my life, and the way I spend my time are some people's dream. I'm either flying to the Bahamas or to my office in Jamaica, or I'm in Miami tending to my offices there. I'm in a business that nobody chose for me, but it's tailor made for me. It pulls from my strengths as a high-level bullshitter and communicator. I was introduced to real estate by a man named Tony when I was 16 years old. He said you could make as much or as little money as you wanted. It all depended on you. Boy, was he right.

It's this business that's given me what I want—the freedom to enjoy my family, to go on some crazy adventures and meet people that I never would have otherwise. This is a beautiful business if you want to hustle and understand that if you don't hunt, you don't eat. As a broker who has interviewed thousands of wannabe agents, I could tell the ones who are just not used to hunting immediately. These are people that are used to food being brought to them and never having to go out there and get it for themselves. These are people that usually have a hard time transitioning into this business.

The real estate business can give you anything you want, but you need to be your own boss. You need to have the discipline to wake up in the morning and set your own priorities and goals. This is not a business for lazy people. Lazy people do not last.

MY FEAR OF SHARKS

My journey starts with 3-year-old me sitting in the front of that shrimp boat with my parents, looking out at a very dark ocean somewhere between Cuba and the US. My parents are having a conversation about dropping me into the water. They were kidding, of course, but they were talking about the sharks eating me. Little did I know that I would spend the rest of my life worrying about sharks—not the actual fish, but the sharks that come at you through life. Those sharks that become obstacles, that need to be overcome to get to where you need to go. Our biggest obstacle was getting to this country, fighting to climb out of poverty and make a better life. That was the first of many sharks I faced along the way.

YOU CAN'T LET YOUR SURROUNDINGS DICTATE WHO YOU WANT TO BE

Don't let your environment paint the picture of who you are going to be. I always knew, growing up poor in the trailer park, that was not who I was. This was not who I wanted to be. I wanted more out of my life, and knew that hard work was going to get me there. It's important to not get captured by that environment and the sharks that patrol those waters. I had a couple close calls on this. I had four run-ins with the law, two of them extremely serious. One of them was a pretty serious cultivation of marijuana charge that could have put me in jail or in prison for a very long time at the age of 19.

I think back now on how lucky I was, because the judge gave me a huge break. I lived in Gainesville, Florida, and there's probably not a Cuban in a hundred-mile radius. But I was lucky enough that the judge was married to a Cuban lady, and he noticed I was born in

Cuba. He also noticed that, when I was in court for my sentencing, my parents were next to me. And he told me, "You should be ashamed of yourself. I know what your people do to come to this country and the hard work that they put in. You are doing what you're doing now, putting shame to your family. And I'm going to give you a chance to show who you can be."

That judge gave me a very light sentence, which basically changed my entire life.

There was another incident where I got in a physical altercation with a police officer. This was another time my environment almost got me, specifically the people I grew up with and was hanging around. This, too, would have put me in prison for a very long time, and once you're in prison, you never know what's going to happen in there. I realized that you need to put yourself and your thoughts where you want to be, not where you physically are. In the house, car, plane, family, and life you want. Don't let the sharks of your past take you down.

"ALL YOU HAVE IS YOUR WORD AND YOUR BALLS. AND DON'T BREAK THEM FOR ANYBODY."

This is a famous saying that has meant a lot in my life. When it comes to avoiding the sharks in life, you have to realize that people can be the sharks. People will lie, cheat, and steal from you if you're not watching out. Being a person who does what they say and has the balls to stick to what is right, regardless of the cost, is the way to fight them off.

People underestimate how important this is in business. You need to do exactly what you say. In the real estate business, ethics are often lacking, yet being true to your word is everything. The relationships that I've built throughout the years are based on trust that I'm going to do what I say I'm going to do. If, for whatever reason, things have to change, we're going to get on a call and discuss those changes.

Communication is also extremely important. I think that probably one of the most important aspects of success is relationships. And relationships are only created by trust and loyalty. You can't do business with somebody for 20, let alone 30 or 40 years if trust and loyalty aren't involved. There's going to be a lot of opportunities to screw people over to make more money. I see people come and go in this business because they do something shady for money. Those people usually don't last. In this—or *any*—business, if you say you're going to pay somebody a certain amount, you make sure you pay that person what you said you would. Giving up your integrity is one of those temptations that can get you if you don't make up your mind ahead of time.

HOW TO WIN FRIENDS AND INFLUENCE PEOPLE: THERE'S ALWAYS GOING TO BE AN ASSHOLE BETWEEN YOU AND SUCCESS

I can tell you that I've read hundreds of books in my life, and if there was just one book I could keep, it would be Dale Carnegie's *How To Win Friends and Influence People*. The skills learned in this book will get you through the business world and its many sharks. I don't think I've ever been in a deal where I haven't had to cross through at least one asshole to get to success, and, make no mistake, these are sharks that will take you down if you let them.

There's going to be many situations where you have to befriend somebody to get a deal. Dealing with difficult people is a task that's never going to go away. The art of turning them into friends will make you millions of dollars. Understanding how humans work, including body language and the correct words to say and not say, are all things that are going to get you very far in life and in business.

Here's an example that will drill in the point that this is important. If you get pulled over and the police officer starts walking towards your car, you start thinking, *what am I going to say?* A million excuses go through your head. But they are not going to get you anywhere. Instead, use the judo approach. Use the other person's momentum against them. When the police officer pulls up next to your car, you tell him, "You caught me red-handed. You should give me three tickets, not one. You got me."

Don't make any excuses. The officer is expecting them. Just go with their momentum. Usually that's going to disarm them and you'll get a smile and they'll let you go.

Another example is when you're negotiating with someone and they bring the "know-it-all" friend that is there to make your life difficult. Usually, these folks know nothing about the deal, only confuse things, and make everything more difficult. You have two choices. You could either get that person on your side, or you can start arguing with them. What I do is make that person seem like the smartest guy in the room. I focus on that person because they are there to shoot me down. So, I'm going to make sure that when I leave, all they do is say great things about me. And that's how you get the deal.

I do this by engaging in conversation with this person. For example, I might say, "Hey, Bob, how do you know so much? Where did you learn all of this? Hey man, this guy's really good. Wow, this guy's smart. Wow, I'm really learning today." All of those things to elevate that person. Because it'll get to a point that, once you leave, there's nothing else they can say but good things about you, because you just elevated them for 20 minutes and, instead of shooting down their stupid ideas, you just made them seem even smarter in the eyes of the person who brought them. These are just a couple of ideas on why it's important to understand people and the psychology of influencing them.

NOT QUITTING

There are a couple things that really got me where I am today. I was raised to not make excuses, to not blame anything on anybody else, and to take responsibility for my actions and really value courage. Being physically and mentally tough and not taking shit from anybody were things that were instilled in me early on as well. Maybe a little bit too much, when I think about all the fights I got into. But I can tell you that that mental toughness had a lot to do with me surviving the most difficult stage in my life and dealing with the sharks that take the form of quitting and excuses.

That's not to say there weren't many nights where I went to sleep crying, wondering, *Why the hell is this happening? I did everything right. I put in the work, I dedicated myself.* When my friends from my early 20s were out there partying, I was out there grinding, opening my company, putting in the long hours, sacrificing to get where I needed to be.

You see, I never went to college or got a degree in anything. I started my real estate brokerage business very young. I didn't have any business mentors anywhere around to ask, "Hey, what do you think about this?" I was five or six years into the company before I even knew what the word "overhead" was.

I started the company in 2001 and it was doing great. I had several offices and flew on my own plane to all my offices around Florida. I'd wake up in the morning, visit the Tampa and Orlando office, and be back in Miami by the end of the day. So that's where things stood, and then 2008 came along. Now, to understand 2008, for those that didn't live through it, it was the worst real estate collapse in the history of the business. Imagine being a guy who never went to school for this, and you're killing it, and all of a sudden you are staring at what seemed like an obsolete business that was just going to go away. But as I always tell my agents, I never once thought about leaving the business.

No one knew how long it was going to last. Everybody was saying, *Oh, this will be back up and running in a couple of months.* Well, it ended up taking a couple of years. I went from flying my own plane to all my offices to, within a year, rationing out my food, literally buying pasta and wine. Yes, I know wine's not a necessity, but it is when you're stressed out and you need to get through the night and try to sleep. I'd be rationing food, because maybe it was Wednesday and I didn't have a check coming till the next Wednesday, and I needed to make sure the food lasted for the week.

The only real money we could make was doing BPOs (Broker Price Opinions). These were basically cheap appraisals the banks would pay desperate agents to do to save the expense of paying for a real appraisal. The banks were paying us $30 to $50 to do one of these. At that time, it was my mother and my wife doing the reports, and I would drive around and take the pictures of the properties for 50 bucks a pop. To take care of a family on that, you've got to do thousands of those, and that's exactly what we did to survive that time.

To start, I was just trying to keep what I had. Any money that came in went to trying to keep "the stuff." Despite my best efforts, though, all the cars, motorcycles, planes, houses, *everything* either got foreclosed or repossessed at some point. I mean, it was from hero to zero within a year. It was really bad. Eventually, the foreclosures and short sales started coming, but before that, there were some very dark and hungry nights.

Looking back now, I *never*, not even one time, thought of quitting. I did at one point think of getting a job as a bouncer at a club. I'm a pretty big guy and have done martial arts my entire life: boxing, kickboxing, judo. I thought, well, I could get a couple hundred bucks at night just to buy food and pay some bills. But that's about it. The only thing that swayed me that I almost went to was just getting a part time job as a bouncer on the weekends, and I didn't do that because I knew it could get in the way of me doing what was needed to build back the business I never considered letting fail.

That's one of the keys to my success. A lot of people start businesses one foot in and one foot out. Anything you start that way, the second it gets tough, you already have one foot out, so it's easy for the other one to join it. I have friends of mine that, in my 25 years being in real estate, have changed careers 10 times. Now, they're in their mid-40s and 50s and are still changing careers. They're still trying to figure out what they're going to do. All they need to do is stick to one thing and give it everything they have. There is no other option. The second you give yourself a way back, or think, *well, if this doesn't go as it should, I always have that,* you have made failure an option. It's always going to be difficult. There are always going to be times when you wonder, *why did I get into this business?* In my time in real estate I've asked that many times. That's with all the success that I've had.

Early on, you're always going to have lots of those days. Expect them. That's when you need to lace up your boots and say to yourself, "I don't care what's happening to me. I'm going to do whatever I have to do. There is no other option."

That attitude got me through the most severe real estate crash in the history of our country, one where almost 80% of agents went running for the hills, mortgage companies closed everywhere, and 200-year-old banks went out of business. Yet, my little company not only survived, but came out of that other side way stronger. All because I told myself, "I'm not leaving this business no matter what. I am here and I'm going to make it through this. I am going to be one of the only companies to make it through this."

That's the attitude that made the difference. Quitting was never on my mind, and I have to thank myself for the balls that it took to survive that stage in my life.

Yes, dealing with people is important. But I would have to put not quitting and not giving yourself options as the most important thing. If you work hard and you don't quit, nobody can stop you. Consistency, which is basically a fancy word for not quitting, is what's going to get you to the promised land. Most people are going to quit. Most people are going to find excuses. Don't be one of those people. Recognize that shark for what it is, and never let it get you.

CHAPTER 6

Finding Happiness and Peace on the Road to Success

Tim Cadillac

Speaker, Professor, and Author

linkedin.com/in/timothycadillac

facebook.com/tcadillac

Tim Cadillac has spent years helping students find meaningful and happy lives. His journey, from dishwasher in his family business at eight years old to his current role as a college professor, provides him with a unique depth of experience, which is evident in his passion as a keynote speaker and author. Tim is driven in his speaking and writing to help people find a more satisfying and joyful life. He is a co-author of the book *The Roadmap to the American Dream,* as well as of the *ACE Investor Ethics* curriculum. He holds master's degrees in both philosophy and theology from Biola University, and has taught thousands of students in over a hundred philosophy and theology classes. Tim does regular volunteer work with several recovery ministries to support and encourage others to become the fullest, best version of themselves, because every human soul is worthy of finding a flourishing life. Tim currently works remotely as a philosophy and ethics professor for a nursing college and lives in Phoenix with his daughter.

"**T**his is it. This is what life will be like from now on."

That is what I thought as I sat slumped in a wheelchair, unable to raise my head, staring at the bottom of the vomit bucket they gave me. Then, I threw up again for the fortieth time in an hour. It was another vertigo attack. I had lost count of how many attacks I had since leaving college my sophomore year for illness. Life had not gone as planned. It did not take long in my journey to realize peace and happiness did not depend on plans going well, health, or wealth. Instead, acceptance and surrender of what I cannot control, taking responsibility for myself and what I believe, and a spirit of gratitude are the ingredients that lead to a fulfilled life.

Two years before finding myself in a wheelchair, my brother and mom looked at me in stunned silence when I said, "I am going to college in Tennessee."

This was unthinkable: leaving the family business in Florida for college in Tennessee. No longer uncoordinated and overweight, I was 23 years old with 230 pounds of muscle, hardworking, intelligent, and ready to excel at college. I believed this new adventure would lead to realizing my American dream. I would find a girl, become an athlete, graduate with honors, and become a successful professional. If I stuck to my plan, pushed through adversity, and reached my goals, happiness was guaranteed.

After a year and a half of running out hard every drill in every practice, my college baseball coach called me to the coach's table in the cafeteria and said, "We've seen your progress, and we want you to pitch for us this season. All we need to see is you pitch in the last intrasquad game on Friday."

This was it. I was finally going to get to play in a game. The truth was, I only made the team because the program was just two years old, and they needed bodies. When I started throwing, I had no idea where the ball was going. However, I worked hard to improve. Now, I had my shot, and in just two days I planned to make the most of it.

The next day, I felt like I had the flu, so I went to the training room. The trainers told me there was nothing they could do for me. They recommended Nyquil and rest. Tomorrow was the big day, so I took the meds and got to bed early. If I stuck to the plan and pushed through, everything would be okay, and I would be one step closer to being happy.

The following morning, I felt better. It was about a 300-yard walk to my first class. At the time, I was in excellent shape, running three miles three times a week, sprinting twice a week, and practicing every weekday. Despite it being a cool Tennessee day, I began to sweat and get short of breath. I told myself, *Everything will be fine. I need to push through, get to class, sit down, and calm my breathing.* When I arrived, I sat down and tried to regulate my breathing.

I realized it wasn't working, so I told myself, *All right, all you need to do is walk the 400 yards to the training room, and they will help you.* I began walking down the hall. After 25 yards, I was having trouble walking steadily. It felt like the hallway was moving. I saw our right fielder walking toward me from the opposite end of the football-length hallway. With a worried look, he yelled out, "Are you okay?"

I couldn't answer; it took all I had to keep walking. After 35 yards, I couldn't walk straight. At 50 yards, I collapsed. I couldn't stand and began sobbing uncontrollably. The next thing I knew, people were calling for an ambulance. Life would never be the same. However, I still believed I could persevere my way to happiness. All I needed to do was get better.

"You've lost a lot. Loss of this magnitude usually results in depression. You should probably go to a therapist."

My doctor's words hit me in the face like a two-by-four a few weeks after my collapse. I was having vertigo attacks every few days, lasting four or five hours. The attacks were exhausting. I would go sheet white, lose all sense of balance, writhe in pain from excruciating pressure in my head, often vomit dozens of times, and feel like I was endlessly falling. I had chronic fatigue, chronic muscle pain, and brain fog, and was diagnosed with incurable chronic vertigo. Too ill to continue at college, I left after my sophomore year, thinking I would not return. My plan was derailing, and now I needed to see a psychologist. In my family, we didn't see therapists. They were for weak people. My father was a member of the Greatest Generation. He taught me that every problem can be overcome by careful planning, lowering your head, and pushing through. Mental toughness could see me through. I wasn't going to accept my current circumstances.

After a year of exhausting all of western medicine's options without progress, I started doing acupuncture. The following summer, my energy improved to 60% of what a regular 26-year-old's would be, and I was ready to return to school. Before returning to college, I attended a three-month academic program, dramatically altering my life's trajectory. I was always a very religious person, but I was experiencing an existential crisis about how to trust God amid tremendous suffering. My professor patiently walked with me through all my hard questions. This helped me make my faith my own and showed me I had good reason to have hope that all my suffering had meaning and purpose. My faith became my lifeline on the hard road ahead. This professor transformed my life in a powerful way when I was in deep turmoil and inspired me to be a teacher. I found my calling to help others. I just had to push through enough school and find a great job. Then, I could find rest, peace, and happiness.

Over the following years, my health stabilized. I ground my way through school and graduated. I almost fell off the graduation stage due to a mild vertigo attack, but I made it. A year before graduating, I married a beautiful girl. I just needed a job, a home, and a family. Getting a job proved difficult, so starting a family was firmly on the back burner. I finally got a teaching job with terrible hours and low pay. It turns out that teaching isn't for the chronically ill. Working 60 to 80 hours a week negatively impacted my health, leading to vertigo attacks and constant exhaustion. I barely saw my wife and medical bills racked up, negatively impacting our marriage. Realizing how bad things were, we decided to risk going to graduate school to invest in a better future. After all, things could not get much worse. I would reach the promised land if I could hold on for three years of graduate school.

We packed up and headed to California. I was accepted to one of America's most rigorous graduate programs in philosophy. It was going to be a fantastic adventure. On the way to California, with our bank account near zero, our tire blew out, our windshield had to be replaced, and I discovered at 31 years old that I was the proud new owner of a cataract in my right eye. Then classes started; they were far more challenging than anything I had experienced or expected. However, one professor encouraged us, saying, "Don't worry, the fog will clear by March."

The only problem was it was the fall semester, and I needed a high GPA to get into a PhD program to achieve my goal of becoming a professor.

Finally, the years of overwork and illness caught up with me. My chronic pain and fatigue went through the roof. For the first time, I experienced severe depression. After two months, I curled up in a ball in our tub and sobbed uncontrollably. My family flew in and we started aggressively pursuing new treatments. We soon discovered I had been misdiagnosed ten years ago. I really had Lyme disease, which, untreated, had ravaged my body. Expensive treatment followed. Finally, I addressed my mental health and discovered my illness caused a chemical imbalance resulting in depression. I was often in bed, experiencing many vertigo attacks, had another cataract, and, at times, had to crawl to the toilet, being too sick to walk. In four of the eight graduate school semesters, I had to take incompletes and finish over breaks.

Nonetheless, in the spring of 2016, I graduated. At the ceremony, my mother's eyes were full of tears. She showed me in the program that I was the only student graduating with the highest honors in two Master's degrees. I couldn't believe it. It was only by God's grace I made it through the program and I did so well. After a grueling four years, I was finally ready for the happier, more peaceful life I felt I had earned.

Following grad school, I became a high school teacher in Las Vegas. I also moonlighted teaching critical thinking part-time at a local community college. Getting a full-time teaching job without a PhD was almost impossible, but this was a step in the right direction. Between the two jobs, I was teaching 60 to 80 hours a week. I loved it, but still spent a lot of my free time in bed. I soon discovered significant hearing loss in both ears, which resulted in me needing hearing aids at age 35. We had a beautiful baby girl, but my wife felt neglected and abandoned between my work and illness. Years of medical bills left us financially strapped and me anxious.

Finally, after another 14-hour day of teaching, I collapsed at the community college. The pressure of work, family, and finances eventually took their toll. I became more moody, negative, critical, irritable, and difficult to live with. I allowed a lot of resentment and self-pity to build up. I didn't realize that I was frustrated that all my hard work and suffering hadn't yielded the happiness or peace I believed I deserved. I had bet my entire life's satisfaction on circumstances and was miserable as a result.

After three tough years in Vegas, we moved to Phoenix. My wife and I agreed I needed to work part-time and focus on my health. Physically, I started to improve, but mentally, my attitude and outlook remained negative. Nonetheless, in 2019, we bought a condo. Then, I miraculously received a full-time college-level position teaching ethics. Finally, I had a wife, a family, a home, and a job. And guess what? I was still not happy.

The good times were short-lived. My wife soon lost her job. My negativity and irritability eventually contributed to my wife divorcing me. I hit rock bottom. I realized all my efforts hadn't yielded the life I believed I deserved. I was finally ready to take a hard look at the choices I made that brought me to exactly where I didn't want to be.

RECOVERING HAPPINESS AND PEACE

When I hit rock bottom, I was broken and desperate for hope. A friend of mine invited me to a faith-based 12-step recovery program called Celebrate Recovery. Not struggling with substance abuse, I was hesitant to attend. However, I was desperate, so I went.

What I learned there has changed my life. It has shown me that I can have happiness and peace right now, regardless of my circumstances. I don't have to wait to achieve success to be happy. Everything in my life began to improve. I recently participated in a 5k foot race. A physician told me that only a handful of people with Lyme's disease in the United States could finish as well as I did.

My daughter recently asked me, "Daddy, do you ever get angry?"

My brother told me that I am now the happiest he has ever seen me. The truth is, when you change, everything changes. I realized I can enjoy life on the way to success, and these principles will only make life much sweeter. Best of all, I believe these principles can benefit anyone.

The first principle is acceptance. During my twenty years of illness, I denied what was true. I believed I could work my way out of any problem. However, the more I attempted to push through, the sicker I became. You cannot solve a problem by pretending it isn't there. I focused entirely on pushing through to my goals. To do so, I neglected my family, and I neglected my character. As a result, I became the kind of person who could not nurture his dreams or enjoy them when they came true. Dreams achieved at the cost of the dreamer ultimately become nightmares. To deny the stewardship of our character and family is to deny the foundation for long-lasting joy.

Bad beliefs allow us to stay in denial and avoid acceptance. People often don't recognize that beliefs run our lives. My controlling belief was that I would be happy if and when I got "x." I left my well-being up to my circumstances. Unfortunately, circumstances aren't guaranteed. I can do all the right things, but I may not get what I deserve. Hard work puts you in a better position to succeed, but it isn't a guarantee. You must accept that there are some things you cannot control. The more I attempted to control the uncontrollable, the more miserable I made myself.

....

Dreams achieved at the cost of the dreamer ultimately become nightmares.

....

The sooner you identify and practice surrendering control of the uncontrollable, the sooner you will find peace. Peace is the door to consistent happiness. My faith helps with surrender. I can more easily release the illusion of control if someone greater than I is in control. Some non-religious methods of surrender involve meditation or visualization, which allows people to release these burdens. Whatever the method is, it is beneficial to practice letting go of burdens that cannot be carried.

Next, you must take responsibility for yourself. While I didn't make myself sick, I did continue to hold onto bad beliefs that negatively impacted my character. I allowed myself to descend into self-pity. Self-pity is rooted in the prideful assumption that I deserve better. This bad belief kept me firmly focused on what I didn't have. Whatever you focus on, you will be drawn towards. I was pulled toward resentment and dissatisfaction over what I lacked. If you do this, you will be perpetually unhappy, just as I was.

Taking responsibility for your beliefs means you must pay careful attention to which beliefs you have and what results they yield. Just as a baker cannot ignore the quality of their ingredients, you cannot ignore the quality of your beliefs. Bad ingredients ruin bread, just as bad beliefs ruin lives.

One such bad belief was confusing taking responsibility with self-condemnation. I believed the best way to motivate myself to do better when I made mistakes was to beat myself up. This was how I was raised. If you did not meet my father's very high standards, you got in trouble. I had adopted this harsh response to failure. However, I eventually realized being harsh with myself did not help me do better in the long run, and was not necessary for me to take responsibility.

....

Bad ingredients ruin bread, just as bad beliefs ruin lives.

....

I believed fear was the only motivator that could get me to perform. Yet, this wasn't the way I treated my successful students or the many successful people I had managed over the years. I would never browbeat an employee for their mistakes, and I certainly wouldn't bring it up over and over again. Why? Because I know I can motivate people in other, less destructive ways. I cannot consistently tear down a person's self-image and performance and expect to get the best out of them. Yet this is exactly what I was doing to myself. While it is true I made a mistake, it isn't helpful to abuse myself for it. Why would you try to motivate yourself in ways you don't believe get the best out of others?

The final principle is to practice gratitude. You must replace your bad beliefs with good ones if you expect to live a consistent life. Shifting your focus to what you have rather than what you lack will cause you to gravitate toward happiness. Making gratitude lists is an effective way to change your thinking. Daily, write down five to ten things you are grateful for. Studies have shown that people who focus on gratitude are happier than people who focus on happiness. Gratitude is the single best predictor of well-being. Being thankful has even been shown to improve our physical health, including lowering blood pressure.

Gratitude pulls me out of the mindset that my life is unsatisfactory. Gratitude provides the fuel of joy to power the daily motivation that brings success over time. Some wrongly believe contentment will diminish our drive to be successful. This hasn't been my experience. As I lean more into my current life, I am more productive, have more energy than ever, and actively pursue new, exciting projects—for instance, contributing a chapter to a book on finding peace and happiness on the road to success.

My story showed me that I didn't need health or financial success to be happy and have peace. I can have them right now by embracing hope, accepting my circumstances, surrendering what I cannot control, taking responsibility for what I can control, and focusing on what I have rather than what I don't. While some people grind their way to success, I want to suggest that one doesn't need to go through a miserable journey to reach a happy destination. It is okay to enjoy the drive.

CHAPTER 7

In Life, Bad Things Happen. . .

But if you look, something better almost always comes from it.

Raul Rodriguez

Raul F. Rodriguez is the CEO of CREI Holdings, a Miami-based development firm focused on affordable and workforce housing. Since its founding in 1982, CREI has delivered critical housing solutions throughout Miami-Dade County. Under Raul's leadership, the firm has completed several major projects, including Li'l Abner Apartments I and II in Sweetwater, and is now developing Li'l Abner III to further meet housing demands for working families, seniors, and youth.

Raul is also the Founder and CEO of National Health Transport, a non-emergency medical transportation company that has rapidly expanded across Florida. With a commitment to training and service, NHT ensures top-tier patient care and professionalism.

Beyond business, Raul is a passionate philanthropist. In 2009, he launched the Li'l Abner Foundation, offering free educational and cultural programs to over 20,000 Sweetwater residents. The foundation provides scholarships and takes terminally ill children on dream trips to Disney World. Raul also leads the city's annual Thanksgiving Bash, serving meals and joy to thousands.

A graduate of Belen Jesuit Preparatory School and Florida International University, Raul is deeply involved in his community, serving on advisory boards and volunteering as a SWAT police officer and martial arts instructor in Sweetwater.

PERSONAL

People see where I am today and think, *man, I wish I could be him*, but they don't realize all the setbacks I encountered along the road to get here. One of the toughest ones was when I decided to get divorced. The whole world turned its back on me, and it did everything possible to make my life a living hell. Those were tough times. This part of my life makes for the perfect example of the saying "everything happens for a reason." When something bad happens, something even better comes out of it. If it wasn't for everyone—even my family—turning their back on me, I would've never been as driven as I was to succeed and prove everyone wrong.

I truly feel that God never gives you what you want. He gives you the opportunities to make things happen and tests you to see how badly you really want it. I always wanted to be an amazing father to my children, and to be a great businessman, like my father. I didn't want my kids to go through the same childhood I did. Sure enough, God gave me the opportunity to do it. I became a single dad for my first three children, met my existing wife, and had two more amazing kids while simultaneously starting my business.

Starting a business is hard, but starting a business with five kids living under your roof is not for the faint of heart. It was hard, and, many times, I wanted to quit, but I knew I couldn't. You have to take the opportunities God gives you out of the bad things that happen. If I never met my ex-wife, I would not have my three amazing children. If I had never gotten divorced, I would never have met my existing wife or have my two youngest children. Without all of that, I wouldn't be able to enjoy having all five of my children together as one family. I would've never had the life I have now.

NHT

One of the biggest, most devastating moments in NHT's (my company's) history is the day that I lost my single largest client in non-medical transport. It was devastating, and I thought I was going to have to file for bankruptcy. I took that opportunity to pivot and move from non-medical to EMS (Emergency Medical Service) transports, selling all existing non-medical trucks and taking the *risk* of purchasing EMS units. If it wasn't for that bad situation where I lost my largest contract, I would never have pivoted to EMS and become one of the largest providers in South Florida, which basically grew my company by a factor of ten overnight.

Whatever you do in life, make sure it is what you love to do, and you are passionate about it. As long as it is your passion, it is never "work."

Starting your company from zero in an area in which you have no idea what you're doing is very difficult, to say the least. With a strong "why," though, there's nothing that can stop me. My father got sick towards the end of his life and transporting him around was very difficult. My father was about 6'2" and 300 pounds, and my mother was 4'11" and 120 pounds. Transportation in Miami for medical patients was very poor. Memories of my mother calling me, saying that Dad missed his doctor's appointment or that he'd been in the truck for over two hours, are something I will never forget. In honor of him, I decided to start a transportation company.

My father will always be my hero. I admired and loved him more than anything in this world. He deserved

> Whatever you do in life, make sure it is what you love to do, and you are passionate about it. As long as it is your passion, it is never "work."

better, and he got it. He was my first transport shortly before he passed away. The loss of my dad left me very depressed. I didn't know what to do with the business, but something inside of me said to keep it for as long as I could. It was very difficult, as I was still working in real estate while trying to operate a healthcare transportation company and not really knowing anything about it. All I knew was one thing: I was committed to always treating each patient as if they were my father. Slowly, the word got around, and my company grew.

> We have been given one chance at this life. Let's leave the world a bit better than when we found it.

As we grew, larger companies would try to block me or buy me out, and I always said no. In every county that I fought to get into, the competitors would tell me, "Raul, we will never let you in." With *consistency*, we have broken into over 15 counties. Now we have over 110 ambulances, over 500 employees, and are doing over 70,000 transports a year, and it's all been organic growth. Purely by word-of-mouth.

I tell each employee, "Every day you come here and you clock in, close your eyes for one second and think of that person you love the most: your mother, father, or your child. How would you transport them?"

For me, every transport is my dad. Starting NHT was one of the most difficult things I've ever done, but it taught me what it meant to have a strong "why." If you do, nothing will ever stop you.

We have been given one chance at this life. Let's leave the world a bit better than when we found it.

MASTER PROJECT

People have asked me why I have taken on my current master project, which is basically building a small city. I took on this endeavor because, about five years ago—to be exact, February 2020—we were offered a significant amount of money for 110 acres of mobile home park. The sum was roughly 350 million dollars. When I received that offer, I thought this would secure my family's legacy and financial stability for generations to come. There was only one issue: I grew up in that park. My first job was picking up garbage every summer, winter, and spring break in a little golf cart. Then I was promoted to working in the pool area, then working on the trailers, and by the time I was 18, I could assemble the homes myself. In my eyes, the park made me who I am today. When I asked the developer what was going to be done with the tenants, he said, "I will give them whatever the state statute allows, and six months to get out."

After a couple days of thinking about it, I had to decline the offer. I said to myself, *I can't turn my back on the place that made me.* If anybody had to relocate the tenants, it would be me, and I would try to do the best that I can by them. I resolved to not only help the existing tenants but build something unique, something that would make an impact on many more people.

A couple days later, I sat down with my design team and told them I had an idea. We went to a restaurant called La Carreta, off of 107th Ave in Miami, and I flipped over the placemat and drew a design of what I envisioned. When I went to throw it away, they both grabbed it and said, "No, you're going to make this a reality one day."

They made me sign and date it and they signed it, too. They said, "One day, when this becomes reality, we're going to hang this on your wall."

That's where this endeavor began. This will be a transformative project that I know will change not only the city, but the county. I kept on repeating that to myself to make sure I stayed the course, and that I was doing all of this for the right reason. There was no other place in the county where a project had over 5000 units of senior, affordable, and workforce housing alongside over 500,000 sq. ft. of retail, a new hospital, charter school, police department, city hall, hotel convention space, and a new central park for the city. **What has helped me in everything I do is visualizing what I'm planning, then writing it down, and I verbalize it as often as I can. Then I work my ass off to make it a reality.**

LI'L ABNER FOUNDATION

I started the foundation because of my family. My father came to the United States with nothing. When people ask me who my hero is, I always tell them it is my father. To be able to come to another country with different customs, a different language, and start from nothing is something that is astonishing to me. He became a very successful businessman, but he always would tell me a phrase that's stuck with me. **Stay humble and never forget where we came from.**

That's why I started the foundation, naming it after the mobile home park I grew up in. I was very fortunate in life. I was able to see both sides of the spectrum. I was able to see less fortunate children that grew up in hardships, and how lucky I was with the family I had. I never had to struggle for much. So, one day, I said to myself, *What can I do to give back to the community that made me who I am?* I told myself I'd start the foundation. I realized that changing people was impossible, so I was just going to give them opportunities, so they have the choice like I did. I started a tutoring program where I brought honors kids from a local private school and FIU University to tutor children, and also offered sports programs.

The children that came to the program would see other children in suits and ties, since they attended the private school, and older kids that were on scholarship at FIU spending their time there to help them. They started to see that they had more options in life than they might have just seeing kids that were in the park, skipping school, joining gangs, and doing things they shouldn't. I was giving them an option and showing them that they're better than that, and they could do great things. Since the program started, we have over 350 kids participating. Many have been able to get scholarships and some have been able to come back and help the program that helped them.

We expanded our martial arts program and now have trained more than five national champions. They get to see a different type of crowd and how hard work and dedication pays off. I thought that I wasn't doing enough, so I decided to do a mini festival for the community, where I would feed over 3000 people and give over 500 toys to children in the city I love.

Combining NHT and the foundation, I decided to embark on another endeavor: helping those who really had it rough. NHT did a particular type of transport called PEPC, which is for medically fragile children, some of whom are terminally ill, quadriplegic, or have other severe issues. When I was called to go visit one of the centers and help them out at a Christmas event, I was so taken aback that I said to myself, "I have to help these kids somehow. What's the one thing that the kids would love to do?"

The administrator said, "Raul, just like any kid, go to Disney. Obviously, that's impossible with these children, because of all the issues they have. Just the logistics of it would be nearly impossible."

I looked at her and said, "We're going make it possible."

Boy, was I in for a surprise. The logistics, let alone the cost, were exorbitant the first year. I tried so hard to make it happen, but I failed. I took a step back and said, "Well, I'm going to try again next year."

She looked at me and said, "I know you mean well, but it's okay."

The more she said it, the more I wanted to do it. The following year, we did everything possible, and we succeeded. We were able to successfully take 16 children to Disney. Seven years later, we now take 70 children every year, and the goal is to hopefully, one day, close down Disney for a day for all the children in the state.

The one lesson that I've taken from starting the foundation is: we've been given one life. Let's use it to the best of our ability to leave this place a little bit better than we found it.

I've been fortunate in life to be successful in business and to be able to take care of family. One of the truest pleasures in my life is seeing the smiles on these kids' faces, knowing that I was a part of it and feeling that I have a purpose in life.

Push yourself to your limits to always improve and do things outside of your comfort zone. Go after your dreams and never give up.

When I was a child, my father had a significant amount of real estate in Sweetwater, specifically the mobile home park. The police department SWAT team would always ask if they could use empty units or trailers for their training. I was fascinated by watching them train. In my early 20s, I went to the mayor one day and asked him, "How can I try out?"

They all laughed and said, "This is not for you."

I started doing my research and found that news reporters would go through basic SWAT training in order to do a documentary on them. I went back to the mayor and the chief of police and I showed them this. They all laughed and said, "You're persistent, so we're going give you the opportunity, but, just to be clear, we are not going to give you any privileges. To the contrary, we will go even harder on you to prove a point."

I told them, "I will not let you down."

There was a SWAT medic course a couple months later, and I signed up. They were not kidding when they said it was extremely difficult, and they were not going take it easy on me. But no matter what they threw at me, **I kept on pushing forward and never gave up.** In the end, I prevailed. I passed. Afterwards, I went to the police chief and the mayor and asked them, "Now that I've done this, how can I do more?"

They said, "Well, you'll have to go to the police academy."

The next day, I found an auxiliary police academy being held at the City of Miami police academy and I signed up. I worked during the day and went to night school for six months. Everybody thought that I was crazy. I graduated from the police academy and I officially began as a Sweetwater police officer. They allowed me to stay on as a reserve officer and be on the SWAT team as long as I put in my hours on the road and went to all the training.

That was one of the happiest times in my life, believe it or not. The camaraderie, the teamwork, the fact that you knew you were doing good and you were with individuals that were willing to give their lives for you, and you for them, is unexplainable. You must go through it to really understand. I would always tell the guys, "It's an honor and privilege to be here."

Being in the police department, I started studying Krav Maga and was able to train in Israel for 72 hours in a no food or sleep survival course in the desert. I also had the opportunity to do the SEALFIT's Kokoro camp. That tested me beyond anything else—48 hours of no sleep and constant physical torture, but I succeeded again. However, one year, when I thought I was in the best shape of my life, I failed. I didn't have the right mindset. I kept asking myself, *Why am I doing this again?* I learned a key lesson: **never lose your why.**

I also learned about Wim Hof, went to his home in Poland, and did many of his training activities, including climbing Kilimanjaro in 48 hours, shirtless, with only shorts. It was only possible because of my brothers who pushed me through the hardest moments.

The most powerful lesson I learned in this is never underestimate the task at hand. Be confident you have your strong "why," and trust in your team.

There is no such thing as "I did it all by myself." Someone along the way helped. Acknowledge them and say, "thank you." It will make you a better person.

The ventures that succeeded for me are the ones where I never gave up. I pushed through the hardest times with consistency and discipline, setting long-term goals and breaking them down into daily wins. People overestimate what they can do in a day, and underestimate what they can do in ten years.

I have one last piece of advice I have learned on love and leadership. In every team, someone leads. Decide who that will be—but lead with integrity, love, and purpose.

So there you have it. That's my story. What strikes me as I look back at it is just how many of the best things I have are the result of coming out on the other side of setbacks. I only needed the willingness to persevere and find something better on the other side of it. There is a great, relevant quote from Thomas Edison that says, "*The one surefire way to succeed is to always just try one more time.*"

CHAPTER 8

Hone Your Superpower: Unlock Your Genius and Crush Your Goals with Ease

Knolly Williams

The Business Healer

Knolly.com

youtube.com/user/knollytraining

linkedin.com/in/knolly

instagram.com/knolly.williams

Knolly Williams, also known as *"The Business Healer,"* is a bestselling author, international speaker, and thought leader who has mastered the art of working smarter—not harder. He runs three thriving six-figure businesses while working just **three hours a day**—and he teaches thousands of entrepreneurs and business leaders how to do the same.

Knolly is the author of the game-changing book, **3 Hours a Day: How Entrepreneurs Can Multiply Their Income by Working Less and Living More** (McGraw Hill). In it, he shares his proven blueprint for building a highly profitable business by focusing solely on your unique genius, eliminating time-wasting activities, and creating systems that work—so you don't have to.

With over 40 years of entrepreneurial experience, Knolly has built multiple six- and seven-figure businesses from the ground up. In his 20s, he launched a seven-figure record label. By his 30s, he became one of America's top real estate brokers, selling over 1,000 homes as a solo agent in just 10 years. In his 40s, he hit the seminar circuit, speaking in over 100 cities worldwide.

Today, Knolly is a real estate broker based in Austin, TX. He inspires tens of thousands through his YouTube channel, the **Mentorship Masters Real Estate Group**, the **Knolly Coaching Club**, and **Life Unlimited Ministries Inc.**—a 501(c)(3) nonprofit dedicated to helping people uncover their God-given passion and purpose.

Through his faith-based teaching, Knolly empowers individuals to discover God's perfect will for their lives and step boldly into their calling—so they can live the extraordinary, fulfilled life they were created for.

FINDING MY SUPERPOWER AT A FLEA MARKET

I discovered the power of a *superpower* when I was just twelve years old, standing in the middle of a bustling flea market. Every weekend, my dad and I would set up a little booth to sell his handcrafted jewelry. The air was hot and thick with the smell of kettle corn and funnel cakes, and the aisles buzzed with families hunting for bargains. At first, I was just a shy kid helping my dad. I'd quietly straighten the displays or fetch items from the back.

One Saturday, something clicked. A woman paused at our table, admiring a turquoise necklace my dad had made. My dad was busy with another customer, so it was up to me to make the sale. Heart pounding, I stepped up and started talking to her—explaining how the necklace was made and how the turquoise color would bring out her eyes. To my surprise, her face lit up, and she bought it on the spot with a big smile.

In that moment, I felt a spark of pure joy. It was the thrill of connecting with someone and helping them get what they wanted. I realized I *loved* this process of selling and interacting; it came easily to me, even though I was just a kid.

That summer, at the flea market, I got hooked on my first business "high." I wasn't the strongest or the loudest kid, but I had a knack for understanding what customers wanted and matching them with the perfect item. I could see even then that this was a special talent—my first glimpse of my innate superpower. It felt *natural* and fun, not like work at all.

While other kids were mowing lawns or playing video games, I was learning how to pitch products and read people's body language. I didn't have the term for it back then, but now I know I was operating in my *zone of genius.* Selling and entrepreneurship lit me up inside, whereas tasks like making the jewelry (which my dad excelled at) didn't excite me as much.

This early experience taught me a lesson I carry to this day: *you have certain gifts that set you on fire*, and when you tap into those, work becomes play and success flows with ease.

EVERYONE IS A GENIUS AT SOMETHING

UNLOCK YOUR GENIUS

There's a popular saying often attributed to Einstein: *"Everybody is a genius. But if you judge a fish by its ability to climb a tree, it will live its whole life believing it is stupid."*

Think about that for a second. How many of us entrepreneurs have felt "stupid" or inadequate just because we struggled while trying to follow someone else's path? Maybe you've looked at another business owner who's killing it on social media through making videos and thought you had to do the same, even though you feel awkward on camera. Or you've seen an extroverted networker going to three events a week and thought, *gee, I guess I need to glad-hand like that to succeed,* even if you're introverted and dread small talk.

We've all been there, trying to climb someone else's tree like a fish out of water. And let me tell you, it never works out well. I spent *years* trying to imitate various mentors and business idols before I learned the truth: every personality type and every individual can succeed, but only by leveraging their own unique strengths.

In other words, you have to do *you.*

The fact is, *you are a genius at something.*

Once you identify that zone of genius, that special ability that comes easily to you and produces great results, you've struck gold. That's your superpower to hone. And here's some good news: you don't have to figure this all out blindly.

There are tools to help you pinpoint your innate strengths. For example, the DiSC assessment can reveal whether you're more Dominant, Influencing, Steady, or Conscientious—insights into how you lead, communicate, and take action.

Likewise, CliftonStrengths (formerly StrengthsFinder) can give you your top talent themes, like Achiever, Empathy, Strategic, or Communication. When I first took these kinds of assessments, I had so many "aha" moments. Traits I used to undervalue in myself suddenly showed up as my top strengths. It was like getting permission to focus on what I naturally do well instead of fixating on what I *thought* I lacked.

When you start operating from your sweet spot, you'll find that you can achieve far more with much less effort. You'll also stop feeling "less than" just because your style or approach is different from the next entrepreneur's. In fact, your unique style *is* the winning path—you just have to own it.

THE 95/5 RULE: DO LESS, ACHIEVE MORE

Let's talk about hustle culture for a second.

You've heard the mantra: *"Rise and grind! 24/7! Sleep when you're dead!"*

The idea is that doing more is the key to success—more hours, more projects, more everything.

Well, I'm about to tell you the opposite: doing less (but the *right* less) is what actually moves the needle.

How is that possible?

It comes down to what I call the 95/5 rule. The 95/5 rule is an extreme spin on the old 80/20 principle. It suggests that roughly 5% of what you do is driving 95% of your results, and the other 95% of your activities are only producing 5% of your outcomes. In other words, a tiny fraction of your efforts yields almost all the benefits. That sounds wild, but in my experience, and that of many entrepreneurs I coach, it holds true. There are a few key actions—your *superpowered* actions—that make all the difference.

The rest is mostly noise that can be minimized, delegated, or dumped.

When I first applied the 95/5 rule to my own business, it was revolutionary. I literally sat down and listed every single task I was doing in a week. It was a long list: answering dozens of emails, fiddling with my website design, posting on five different social media platforms, servicing clients, prospecting for new clients, doing bookkeeping, creating marketing materials, attending meetings, on and on.

Then I asked myself: *Which of these activities are actually generating income or driving the business forward?* Also, *which of these activities am I really brilliant at doing or truly enjoy?* The overlap between those two questions pointed to my 5% power activities.

I discovered that my top few activities were: (1) connecting with clients and closing deals, (2) creating content and teaching (since I love to share knowledge), and (3) developing big picture strategies for growth. Those were my superpower zones that directly led to revenue and expansion. A lot of the other stuff—admin work, routine follow-ups, technical chores—were things that either someone else could do, or maybe didn't need to be done as frequently as I was doing them.

So I made a bold decision: I started ruthlessly cutting or delegating the majority of the tasks that weren't in that magic 5%.

I hired a virtual assistant to filter and handle emails, I brought on a part-time bookkeeper for the finances, and I stopped saying yes to meetings that didn't have a clear purpose. It felt strange at first—like, "Wait, can I really only focus on a couple of things and ignore the rest?"

But an amazing thing happened. My productivity and income didn't drop; they *increased.* By pouring my energy into the few things that I do best and that mattered most, I was able to produce higher quality work and close more business than when I was spread thin.

And all those other tasks? They got done by someone else, or they turned out not to be as critical as I had assumed. This is how I eventually got down to working just three hours a day, yet I was multiplying my income in the process. It wasn't about some gimmick or luck. It was the strategic application of the 95/5 rule.

Now, I'm not saying you should literally do only 5% of the work and ignore everything else entirely—especially if you're a solopreneur right now. But you *can* prioritize like crazy.

Identify your version of the 5%. What are the one or two things you could do today that would have the biggest impact on your goals? Do those first. Conversely, identify your time-wasters—the busywork that makes you *feel* productive but isn't moving the needle. Start trimming those.

When you align nearly all your time and effort around your high impact, "genius zone" activities, you'll find you can achieve more in a few focused hours than most people do in days or even weeks of "grind."

It's not about how much you do, it's about doing what counts. Quality over quantity, impact over hours worked. That's the 95/5 rule in action, and it's a total game-changer for crushing your goals with a lot more ease.

WORKING IN EASE AND FLOW

One of the greatest signs that you're honing your superpower and operating in your zone of genius is a feeling of *ease and flow*. Now, "ease" doesn't mean you're kicking back and sipping lemonade while your bank account magically grows—wouldn't that be nice! You still have to put in effort. But ease and flow mean that your work *feels* natural, energizing, and even joyful, rather than forced, draining, or constantly stressful.

It's the difference between swimming *with* the current versus against it. When you're in your genius zone, you're swimming with the current of your talents and passions. You get more done with less effort, and you often enjoy the process.

Time flies during those flow moments—have you experienced that? When you're so immersed in an activity you love that you look up and realize hours have passed without you noticing? That's being in a state of flow, and it's a delicious feeling.

Contrast that with when you're doing something that's *not* in your wheelhouse.

Every minute can feel like an hour. You procrastinate, you dread it, you maybe even physically feel tired at the mere thought of it. That's a sign you're out of alignment with your superpower.

Sure, you have to do some chores in life and business that you may never love, but you want to minimize those. The goal is to design your business life so that as much of it as possible is spent in activities that put you in that flow state.

Not only will you be happier, but you'll also be far more effective.

I used to think "work" by definition had to be hard—and if it felt easy or fun, I must not be doing it right or not working hard enough. Man, what a limiting belief that was! In truth, when you find the courage to trust the ease, you'll see that you can actually *have fun* and kick butt at the same time.

Let me give you a personal example. I'm a teacher at heart. I absolutely come alive when I'm sharing knowledge, whether it's through writing, speaking on stage, or coaching someone one-on-one. I enter a flow state in those moments; I could do it for hours and still have energy.

For a long time, though, I only did that during the breaks in my schedule, because I was "supposed to" be doing traditional grinding tasks, like cold calling leads, eight hours a day. I hated cold calling with a passion; as outgoing as I can be, the script-like dialing drained me. But I did it because I thought I had to hustle that way.

Eventually, I realized that my best clients actually came from workshops and seminars I gave—from teaching, not dialing.

People would hear me speak, trust my expertise, and then want to hire me. And I *loved* those workshops. Ding! The light bulb went off: what if I just did more teaching (my ease and flow activity) and cut back on the tactics that felt like slogging through mud?

The result: my business didn't collapse; it grew. I attracted clients who were aligned with me, and I enjoyed every day so much more.

Don't buy into the myth that success only comes through suffering and strain.

Yes, effort is required, but it can be an *inspired effort*. When you embrace the way God uniquely designed you and lean into activities that feel fluid to you, you'll notice a greater grace in your workflow.

Problems seem to get solved more readily, or you find solutions quicker, because you're functioning in a higher gear.

Operating in ease and flow is a sign you're on the right track. It doesn't mean there won't be challenges—there will, that's life—but you'll face them with more resilience because you're not constantly exhausted and frustrated.

Pay attention to when you feel that flow, and find ways to spend more time there. It's not lazy or indulgent; it's smart. It's like a clue from your soul (and, I believe, from God) saying, "This is what I made you to do—do more of this!"

YOUR TURN: EMBRACE YOUR UNIQUE PATH TO SUCCESS

We've covered a lot in this chapter, so let's bring it all home. The core message I want you to walk away with is this: your greatest success will come from embracing and honing *your* superpower, operating in *your* genius zone, and not trying to live someone else's script.

You have permission to do business in the way that feels right and natural to you. In fact, not only do you have permission—you have a mandate.

The world needs your authentic contribution. There are people out there who will benefit uniquely from the way *you* do things, the way you solve problems, the way you bring your personality into your work. If you hide that by trying to copy someone else, the world misses out and so do you.

So here's my call to action for you: take one concrete step in the next 24 hours to align more with your superpower.

Maybe that means finally taking that personality or strengths assessment and reflecting on the results. Or having a brainstorming session to list out what you really love in your business as opposed to what you've been doing because you feel you "must."

It could mean starting your own list and pinpointing one task to delegate or drop this week.

Perhaps it's reaching out to a mentor, coach, or trusted friend and saying, "Hey, I'm trying to get clarity on what I'm truly great at and enjoy—what do you see in me?" Sometimes others see the light in you better than you do yourself.

If you're a person of faith, spend some time in prayer, asking God to show you opportunities to use your gifts more fully, and to give you the courage to step out in faith on the path He's nudging you toward.

As you take these steps, commit to a mindset shift: from this day on, no more beating yourself up for what you're not. Celebrate what you *are*. No more wearing masks to try to impress some imaginary jury of "successful people."

You're going to carve your own path. It might be different, it might even be contrary to the mainstream advice, but if it resonates with your soul and leverages your strengths, it's the right path. Trust that. I often say, ease is the new hustle. That means flowing in your God-given genius is the new working your fingers to the bone.

Working smarter *and* with joy is the new badge of honor.

Imagine a future where you wake up excited because you know the day ahead is filled with activities you love and do well. You have a team or systems handling the rest, and you've got time to spend with your family, to travel, to learn new things—all because you're not bogged down in the muck of overwhelm. You're achieving your goals, crushing them even, and it feels almost *effortless* at times.

That future is possible.

I know because I'm living it, and I've seen others live it, too.

If a scared kid peddling jewelry at a flea market can transform into a thriving entrepreneur who works three hours a day doing what he loves, why not you?

The journey won't be without challenges, but now you have some tools and insights to help you navigate: focus on your 5% super-tasks, build your iceberg foundation beneath the surface, follow the ease and flow, use your list of strengths to guide your daily activities, and anchor yourself in faith and purpose.

Clarity and joy are your companions when you align with your unique design.

As I close this chapter, I want to leave you with this empowering thought: *You were created with a specific genius that the world needs, and you thrive when you operate in it.*

Success with ease is not a fairy tale; it's a choice to trust your gifts, work hard on the right things, and let go of the rest.

Your superpower is waiting to be fully unleashed. Hone it, embrace it, and run with it. The entrepreneurial journey becomes an odyssey of growth and fulfillment when you travel it as your authentic, genius self.

So go ahead—unlock your genius and crush your goals with ease. The world is waiting to see you, the *real* you, succeed. Now, get out there and harness your superpower like the hero you were born to be!

You've got this.

CHAPTER 9

Overcoming Constant Fear

Craig Grant

CEO of the Real Estate Technology Institute/RETI |
Co-Founder of the BEATS Alliance & BEATS Conference
International Speaker, Trainer, and Tech Evangelist

craiggrant.info

reti.us

beatsconference.com

facebook.com/craiggrantreti

Craig Grant is the lead Subject Matter Expert (SME) of the National Association of REALTORS' (NAR) recent rebuild of ePro certification and an RISMedia Newsmaker as an Industry Futurist. With over 150 in-person and virtual speaking engagements around the world each year, including sessions for NAR, several state conventions, franchises, CRS, REBI, and other key industry events, he is considered one of the most sought-after technology, marketing, and cybersecurity speakers around.

Whether it be at an industry event, in the classroom, or online via Zoom or the RETI.us portal, one thing that fuels Craig is helping today's real estate professionals embrace and get over their fear of technology so that it can work *for* them, not against them.

As stated in his motto, "Advanced Real Estate Technology & Marketing Instructed at a Pre-K Level," Craig is able to take extremely complicated topics and present them in a way that the average non-technical person not only understands but is able to apply to improve their business.

In addition to being the CEO of the Real Estate Technology Institute and RETI.us, the Real Estate Industry's Home for Online Technology Education, Craig Grant is an avid sports fan and music lover who can be found watching or participating in events and concerts with friends.

• • •

F ear. Fear is a word that can mean many different things to different people.

For some, it took the form of:

- The bully who terrorized the schoolyard, who kept you up late at night, dreading going to school the next day.
- That rattling noise that you were sure was just the furnace, but you still didn't want to go down to the basement to investigate it.
- The time in your life when you had to leave the nest, graduate into adulthood, and strike out on your own.
- The moment you feared the most, hearing devastating news about yourself or someone you loved.

However, for some people, fear is not simply an emotion associated with a singular moment or period of time. It is a constant. When a fear becomes a constant, it typically doesn't happen overnight. It often builds up over time, earned after years of repeated failures or embarrassment. Once that callus builds up, it can become so ingrained and debilitating, to the point of paralysis, that you try to avoid that activity, expending energy in the form of aversion rather than investing the time and effort it may require into overcoming your fear.

But what happens when that exact thing you have a constant fear of becomes central to succeeding in today's society, and both your personal and professional livelihoods may depend on it?

Well, for many people, that is exactly what has happened over the last 25+ years. Technology, the Internet, mobile devices, social media, and now Generative AI have taken over just about every aspect of today's world. It has become so prevalent that you can't really function as a person, and especially in business, without a good grasp of the exact thing you may have grown to hate and fear.

I try my best not to stereotype things, as I have run into many seniors who are flat-out tech geniuses and many younger people who are tech noobs. That said, when it comes to technology, it is often true that for many from generations that didn't grow up with the Internet or a computer in their back pockets, or using social media or AI, modern technology can be a common and significant source of fear.

As a professional speaker, trainer, and coach who specializes in cutting-edge technologies, such as artificial intelligence, digital marketing, tech trends and usage, and cybersecurity, a core part of my job is to teach people how to use and leverage technology in their daily lives and business, and inspire them to do so. This includes a good percentage of those who attend each of my events, who may have a strong constant fear of the exact thing I am challenged with leading them through, and, on top of that, I carry the burden of knowing that many of them are there because they know they *have* to be there, if they want a chance to survive and thrive in many areas of modern life. In other words, they see me as their last hope to help them overcome their constant fear of technology.

And the craziest part is I typically don't have the liberty of being able to coach and monitor these people on a daily or ongoing basis. I've got to pull this off in just a few hours, often to a large crowd (where I don't even get to engage with each person on an individual level), and to thousands of people a year.

My goal for this chapter is to share with you what I feel is my secret sauce, or the keys and processes I've utilized for the last more than 20 years to help thousands of people break through their constant fear of technology. Hopefully, it can help you (or someone you love or manage) get out of neutral and to that next level or stage, conquering that constant fear, whether it be technology or anything else that haunts you or holds you back from truly succeeding in life or business.

To start, one of the key things I've discovered after years of watching this dynamic unfold in rooms big and small, filled with people from all walks of life, is that fear isn't just a feeling—it's often a belief system we've unknowingly accepted as truth. It's the internal dialogue or voice in your head that says, "I'm too old for this," "I'll never be able to understand this," "I have always had an aversion to this and if anyone can break it, it will be me," or "What if I mess up and everyone sees?"

These aren't just hesitations—they're defense mechanisms that you've built up over years of consistent failure or humiliation, also known as a *constant fear*. If left unchecked, this *constant fear* can create walls. And, as mentioned previously, these walls build up and strengthen over time, to the point where they can have serious implications for how you are able to live your life or succeed in business.

> **Fear isn't just a feeling—it's often a belief system we've unknowingly accepted as truth.**

At every event I speak at, I can see these people in my crowds, sometimes even in the front row of my sessions, with arms crossed and jaws clenched, clearly dreading the next slide, thinking: *"This tech stuff is just not for me,"* or *"Why am I here?"* And yet, by the end of the session, some of those same people are the ones who walk up to me, almost in disbelief, saying things like, "I never thought I'd say this, but I'm actually excited to try this out," "You know, I seriously didn't want to come here today, but I am so glad I did," or "Not sure how you did it, but I think I finally understand and feel confident enough to go home and apply this to my life or business."

So, how does that transformation happen?

Am I some kind of magician who was able to lift the cloud of doubt and dispel their *constant fear* from their lives? Well, I do like to fashion myself as a bit of a wizard at times, but in this case, it's not magic at all. It starts by creating an open environment that is comfortable for all, no matter what their knowledge or skill level is. But even more importantly, I lead with compassion and focus on reframing the very concept of fear so that everyone in my crowd feels seen and heard.

REFRAMING FEAR

One of the most powerful tools I've used in my own life—and shared with others—is a reframing of the word *fear* that turns it into a more gentle acronym:

F.E.A.R. = False Expectations Appearing Real

Aside from the fact that it is less abrasive, that phrase hits hard for a reason. Because most of the time, what we fear isn't the thing itself, it's the *story* we've told ourselves about it. It's the story that says technology is only for the young. That failure is something to be avoided at all costs. That asking for help makes you weak.

> Will you let fear freeze you—or fuel you?

But what if, instead of retreating, we leaned in? What if, instead of letting *constant fear* define us, we used it to refine ourselves?

I see this pattern not just with technology, but with people trying to start a business, get in shape, recover from a loss, or step up as leaders. Fear may be part of the process, but it doesn't have to be the end of the story.

The beautiful truth is: **every single breakthrough begins where fear tries to stop you.** And when you realize that your fear is often based on an illusion, or the story you've told yourself, and is not rooted in fact, you take the first step toward overcoming your constant fear and, thus, freedom.

So whether it's tech, public speaking, building a brand, or simply believing in yourself again after life knocked you down... it all comes back to a choice: Will you let fear freeze you—or fuel you?

THE FOUR-STEP BREAKTHROUGH FRAMEWORK: FROM FEAR TO FORWARD MOTION

After working with thousands of professionals, entrepreneurs, and everyday people over the last two decades, I've realized that helping someone overcome their constant fear, especially fear of technology, requires more than just information. It requires that person to go through a transformation.

And transformation isn't magic. It's a process. I call this one my "Breakthrough Framework," built around four key steps:

1. ACKNOWLEDGE THE FEAR WITHOUT JUDGMENT

You can't conquer what you won't confront. Whether someone admits, "I'm terrible with tech," or says "I'm just not wired for this," I always affirm one thing first: it's okay to feel afraid. Fear is human. What matters is what you do with it. So, just like anything else in life, the first step in being able to fix or overcome something is to acknowledge or come to terms with whatever is causing the problem. The key is to do it without fear of judgment or embarrassment by others.

This is where most people go wrong—they either shame themselves or hide behind excuses. But when you acknowledge your fear without judgment, you create space to grow beyond it.

2. REFRAME THE NARRATIVE

Once you have identified the source of your constant fear and it is on the table, the next step is to dismantle the stories you've told yourself about it. For example, instead of thinking, *I'm too old for this*, ask yourself, *What if my experience gives me a unique advantage once I master this tool?* Instead of, *I'll never get it*, ask yourself, *What's one small thing I could learn today to build momentum or help me start overcoming this constant fear?*

Remember, words shape reality. When you rewrite the story you've been telling yourself all this time, you effectively reshape your response, and you will be on your way to overcoming this constant fear.

3. SIMPLIFY THE FIRST STEP

This is where most "experts" fail. They overwhelm their audience with jargon, features, and theories. I take the opposite approach: I try to break things into ridiculously simple, confidence-building wins.

Can you open the app and log in? Perfect. Can you send one email? Great. Can you post your first video—even if it's just 10 seconds? Awesome, you're already ahead of most people.

For every mini-win you tally on your mental scorecard, it starts tearing down those walls you've built over time, and now we can start chipping away at that constant fear. Fear loses its grip when progress is visible and nerve-wracking tasks become doable.

4. CELEBRATE PROGRESS RELENTLESSLY

Confidence doesn't come from perfection—it comes from proof. Every time you face a fear and push through, you deserve to celebrate it. I don't care how small the step is. Progress is power.

Give yourself small, easily attainable goals that will give you many and frequent opportunities to complete, accomplish, and celebrate.

Whether it's clapping for yourself after creating your first social media profile, giving yourself a gold star, or sharing a "win of the week" in a group, celebrating success reinforces the belief that *"I can do this."*

KEEPING THE FLAME ALIVE: HOW TO MAINTAIN MOMENTUM AFTER A BREAKTHROUGH

Breakthroughs are powerful—but by themselves, they're not enough. Ask anyone who's ever made a New Year's resolution or left a motivational event feeling unstoppable, only to find themselves back in the same rut weeks later.

That's because breakthroughs are igniters, not engines.

To sustain momentum, you need something more durable than adrenaline. You need structure, support, and systems that turn inspiration into consistent action.

Here are five strategies I teach to help people reach their goal of defeating their constant fear and then stay on track long after the initial fear has been conquered:

1. ANCHOR YOUR PROGRESS IN A DAILY PRACTICE

Breakthroughs create possibility. *Consistency* creates change.

In some of my sessions, I jokingly tell my attendees to get ready, because I am about to be a firehose of information: they are about to get a slew of amazing tools and tricks that can help them be way more efficient and elevate their business. I warn them that there is no way they will be able to implement everything I am about to cover. Instead, I suggest that they identify two to three of the most relevant items or nuggets of gold that they feel will have the biggest immediate impact on their business, and that they should leave with a goal to implement those top items. Of those, they should attempt one at a time, because the worst thing they can do is leave with a list of 20 and implement none. I encourage attendees at my events to only take on what they can handle, create very realistic and doable tasks, and commit to just 15 to 30 minutes a day of "tech time" or fear-facing action.

Whether they experiment with that by adding a new social media channel into the mix, a new app or tool into their stack, or learning or practicing a new tool, they're not trying to master it all at once. Remember, you have to crawl before you can walk; one thing at a time.

They're simply reinforcing the habit of showing up. Daily action turns the unfamiliar into the unshakable.

2. TRACK YOUR WINS (NO MATTER HOW SMALL)

What gets measured gets managed, and what gets celebrated gets repeated. Remember, we want to celebrate every milestone or achievement, no matter how small it may be.

I often recommend people keep a "Confidence Journal"—a running log of the things they've learned, tech they've tackled, or moments in which they overcame self-doubt. These records become proof of progress when motivation dips.

It's amazing what happens when people flip through that journal and realize, *"I'm not who I was a month ago."* They might still think they have that constant fear, but after seeing and living these achievements, they may see how far they've actually come.

3. CREATE A FEAR-FIGHTING INNER CIRCLE

It's easy to fall back into old patterns if you're surrounded by people who reinforce your old identity.

That's why I encourage people to seek out or create a "growth tribe"—a group of others who are also committed to pushing through their fears and growing their skill sets. Whether it's an accountability partner (friend, family member, spouse, co-worker, etc.), a local mastermind group, or even an online community, such as a Facebook or LinkedIn group, community equals continuity.

Aligning yourself with others who have similar challenges and are trying to grow at the same time as you can be a huge asset in helping you overcome your own constant fear. When you see others overcoming their own fears, it reminds you: *"If they can do it, so can I."*

4. REPLACE PERFECTION WITH CURIOSITY

Fear loves perfectionism. It thrives on the lie, "if you can't do it perfectly, don't do it at all."

The antidote? Curiosity.

Do you know the main differences between a young learner and a senior one? Well, we've already beaten fear into the dirt, as the older we get, the more fearful we get to learn new things, but the other main difference is curiosity. In other words, you task a young person with learning a new skill and they typically jump in right away, start asking questions, Googling or YouTubing it, or figuring it out on their own. In other words, they are driven by curiosity, whereas the senior learning the same skill typically isn't curious and is resistant to change.

To conquer your constant fears, you should approach everything with the mindset of a learner, not a performer. Ask questions. Try things. Mess up and laugh. The more playful your approach, the less power fear has to shame you. When tech—or anything new—becomes a sandbox instead of a spotlight, growth becomes inevitable.

5. MAKE YOUR "WHY" LOUDER THAN YOUR "WHAT-IFS"

Finally, and perhaps most importantly, the people who maintain momentum are the ones who stay deeply connected to *why* they're doing this in the first place. Is it to stay competitive in your field? To connect with your grandkids? To finally launch your dream side business?

When fear whispers, "What if you fail?" your *why* needs to roar back: "But what if I succeed?"

CONCLUSION: FROM FEAR TO FREEDOM

Fear may always be part of the human experience, but it doesn't have to be the author of your story. Whether it shows up as a one-time obstacle or a constant hum in the background of your life, fear is not your enemy—it's your invitation. An invitation to grow. To rise. To break through.

Throughout this chapter, we've explored how constant fear, whether it be the fear of technology or anything that is holding you back in life or business, can become a barrier that feels impossible to overcome. But we've also seen how that same fear, when reframed and faced with intention, can become your greatest teacher, which can help you grow in all aspects of life.

You've learned that:

- Fear is often based on "False Expectations Appearing Real," and when you question those expectations, they begin to dissolve.

- Even a *constant fear* can be decoded and dismantled, step-by-step, into action and empowerment.

- Breakthroughs happen when you reframe your story, take simple steps, and celebrate progress.

- Lasting change is possible when you create daily habits, surround yourself with support, and lead with purpose.

I've watched thousands of people walk into my sessions afraid, overwhelmed, and skeptical—and walk out with a spark. Not just because they learned something new, but because they remembered who they are: capable, adaptable, and worthy of growth.

And now, I hope that same spark is alive in you.

If you take just one thing from this chapter, let it be this:

Fear will visit, but it doesn't get to stay.

Your courage, curiosity, and commitment are stronger.

The moment you decide to stop letting that constant fear dictate your direction is the moment you begin to lead your life with intention, and that is where true success begins.

So go ahead—take the next step.
Not because you're not afraid. . .
But because you finally know you're bigger than the fear.

• • •

Conclusion

T he entrepreneurial journeys shared within these pages offer more than motivation—they provide a mirror. Through diverse industries and life experiences, each contributor in *Success4Life: The Entrepreneur's Odyssey* has revealed a simple but profound truth: success is not a destination to be reached, but a path to be forged.

These narratives illustrate that success, when defined by character, conviction, and contribution, transcends metrics. Whether navigating personal loss, professional reinvention, or industry disruption, these leaders made intentional choices—ones grounded in discipline, adaptability, and purpose.

If a unifying theme emerges, it is this: real success is individual, earned, and aligned with one's values. It cannot be replicated by following another's formula, nor can it be sustained without clarity of vision and consistency of action.

As the reader, you are now invited to reflect: What does success look like for you? What values will shape your journey? What legacy will your work leave?

Let this volume serve not as a conclusion, but as a call—to lead with integrity, to act with purpose, and to write the next chapter of your own odyssey.

Will You Share the Love?

If you've enjoyed *Success4Life*, the authors have a favor to ask.

Would you consider giving it a rating wherever you bought the book? Online book stores are more likely to promote a book when they feel good about its content, and reader reviews are a great barometer for a book's quality.

Also, if you have found this book valuable and know others who would find it useful, consider buying them a copy as a gift. Special bulk discounts are available if you would like your whole team or organization to benefit from reading this. Just contact josh@joshcadillac.com.